I0831182

THE ANALECTS

The Analects

Confucius c. 551 – c. 479 bc
Translated by William Jennings
Published by Colonial Press in 1900
Jennings, William 1847 – 1927

Text set in 18 point Helvetica.
Chapter headings set in Helvetica Neue.

ISBN: 978-1-83412-282-3

THE ANALECTS

CONFUCIUS

Translated into English
by William Jennings

GRAND TYPE CLASSICS

CONTENTS

The Analects

PRONUNCIATION OF PROPER NAMES

j, as in French. **ng**, commencing a word, like the same letters terminating one. **ai** or **ei**, as in **aisle** or **eider**. **au**, as in German, or like **ow** in **cow**. **t'**, as in **fîte**. **i** (not followed by a consonant), as **ee** in **see**. **u** (followed by a consonant), as in **bull**. **iu**, as **ew** in **new**. **ui**, as **ooi** in **cooing**. **h** at the end of a name makes the preceding vowel short. **i** in the middle of a word denotes an aspirate (**h**), as **K'ung**=Khung.

INTRODUCTION

THE STRANGEST FIGURE that meets us in the annals of Oriental thought is that of Confucius. To the popular mind he is the founder of a religion, and yet he has nothing in common with the great religious teachers of the East. We think of Siddartha, the founder of Buddhism, as the very impersonation of romantic asceticism, enthusiastic self-sacrifice, and faith in the things that are invisible. Zoroaster is the friend of God, talking face to face with the Almighty, and drinking wisdom and knowledge from the lips of Omniscience. Mohammed is represented as snatched up into heaven, where he receives the Divine communication which he is bidden to propagate with fire and sword throughout the world. These great teachers lived in an atmosphere of the supernatural. They spoke with the authority of inspired prophets. They brought the unseen world close to the minds of their disciples. They spoke positively of immortality, of reward or punishment beyond the grave. The present life they despised, the future was to them everything in its promised satisfaction. The teachings of Confucius were of a very different sort. Throughout his whole writings he has not even mentioned the name of God. He declined to discuss the question of immortality. When he was asked about spiritual beings, he remarked, "If we cannot even know men, how can we know spirits?"

Yet this was the man the impress of whose teaching has formed the national character of five hundred millions of people. A temple to Confucius stands to this day in every town and village of China. His precepts are committed to memory by every child from the tenderest age, and each year at the royal university at Pekin the Emperor holds a festival in honor of the illustrious teacher.

The influence of Confucius springs, first of all, from the narrowness and definiteness of his doctrine. He was no transcendentalist, and never meddled with supramundane things. His teaching was of the earth, earthy; it dealt entirely with the common relations of life, and the Golden Rule he must necessarily have stumbled upon, as the most obvious canon of his system. He strikes us as being the great Stoic of the East, for he believed that virtue was based on knowledge, knowledge of a man's own heart, and knowledge of human-kind. There is a pathetic resemblance between the accounts given of the death of Confucius and the death of Zeno. Both died almost without warning in dreary hopelessness, without the ministrations of either love or religion. This may be a mere coincidence, but the lives and teachings of both men must have led them to look with indifference upon such an end. For Confucius in his teaching treated only of man's life on earth, and seems to have had no ideas with regard to the human lot after death; if he had any ideas he preserved an inscrutable silence about them. As a moralist he prescribed the duties of the king and of the father, and advocated the cultivation by the individual man of that rest or apathy of mind which resembles so much the disposition aimed at by the Greek and Roman Stoic. Even as a moralist, he seems to have sacrificed the ideal to the practical, and his loose notions about marriage, his tolerance of concubinage, the slight emphasis which he lays on the virtue of veracity – of which indeed he does not seem himself to have been particularly studious in his historic writings – place him low down in the rank of moralists. Yet he taught what he felt the people could receive, and the flat mediocrity of his character and his teachings has been stamped forever upon a people who, while they are kindly, gentle, forbearing, and full of family piety, are palpably lacking not only in the exaltation of Mysticism, but in any religious feeling, generally so-called.

The second reason that made the teaching of Confucius so influential is based on the circumstances of the time. When this thoughtful, earnest youth awoke to the consciousness of life about him, he saw that the abuses under which the people groaned sprang from the feudal system, which cut up the country into separate territories, over which the power of the king had no control. China was in the position of France in the years preceding Philippe-Auguste, excepting that there were no places of sanctuary and no Truce of God. The great doctrine of Confucius was the unlimited despotism of the Emperor, and his moral precepts were intended to teach the Emperor how to use his power aright. But the Emperor was only typical of all those in authority – the feudal duke, the judge on the bench, and the father of the family. Each could discharge his duties aright only by submitting to the moral discipline which Confucius prescribed. A vital element in this system is its conservatism, its adherence to the imperial idea. As James I said, "No bishop, no king," so the imperialists of China have found in Confucianism the strongest basis for the throne, and have supported its dissemination accordingly.

The Analects of Confucius contain the gist of his teachings, and is worthy of study. We find in this work most of the precepts which his disciples have preserved and recorded. They form a code remarkable for simplicity, even crudity, and we are compelled to admire the force of character, the practical sagacity, the insight into the needs of the hour, which enabled Confucius, without claiming any Divine sanction, to impose this system upon his countrymen.

The name Confucius is only the Latinized form of two words which mean "Master K'ung." He was born 551 B.C., his father being governor of Shantung. He was married at nineteen, and seems to have occupied some minor position under the government. In his twenty-fourth year he entered upon the three years' mourning for the death of his mother. His seclusion gave him time for deep thought and the study of history, and he resolved upon the regeneration of his unhappy country. By the time he was thirty he became known as a great teacher, and disciples flocked to him. But he was yet occupied in public duties, and rose through successive stages to the office of Chief Judge in his own country of Lu. His tenure of office is said to have put an end to crime, and he became the "idol of the people" in his district. The jealousy of the feudal lords was roused by his fame as a moral teacher and a blameless judge. Confucius was driven from his home, and wandered about, with a few disciples, until his sixty-ninth year, when he returned to Lu, after accomplishing a work which has borne fruit, such as it is, to the present day. He spent the remaining five years of his life in editing the odes and historic monuments in which the glories of the ancient Chinese dynasty are set forth. He died in his seventy-third year, 478 B.C. There can be no doubt that the success of Confucius has been singularly great, owing especially to the narrow scope of his scheme, which has become crystallized in the habits, usages, and customs of the people. Especially has it been instrumental in consolidating the empire, and in strengthening the power of the monarch, who, as he every year burns incense in the red-walled temple at Pekin, utters sincerely the invocation: "Great art thou, O perfect Sage! Thy virtue is full, thy doctrine complete. Among mortal men there has not been thine equal. All kings honor thee. Thy statutes and laws have come gloriously down. Thou art the pattern in this imperial school. Reverently have the sacrificial vessels been set out. Full of awe, we sound our drums and bells."

E. W.

The Analects

BOOK ONE

On Learning – Miscellaneous Sayings: –

"TO LEARN," said the Master, "and then to practise opportunely what one has learnt – does not this bring with it a sense of satisfaction?

"To have associates in study coming to one from distant parts – does not this also mean pleasure in store?

"And are not those who, while not comprehending all that is said, still remain not unpleased to hear, men of the superior order?"

A saying of the Scholar Yu: –

"It is rarely the case that those who act the part of true men in regard to their duty to parents and elder brothers are at the same time willing to turn currishly upon their superiors: it has never yet been the case that such as desire not to commit that offence have been men willing to promote anarchy or disorder.

"Men of superior mind busy themselves first in getting at the root of things; and when they have succeeded in this the right course is open to them. Well, are not filial piety and friendly subordination among brothers a root of that right feeling which is owing generally from man to man?"

The Master observed, "Rarely do we meet with the right feeling due from one man to another where there is fine speech and studied mien."

The Scholar Tsang once said of himself: "On three points I examine myself daily, viz., whether, in looking after other people's interests, I have not been acting whole-heartedly; whether, in my intercourse with friends, I have not been true; and whether, after teaching, I have not myself been practising what I have taught."

The Master once observed that to rule well one of the larger States meant strict attention to its affairs and conscientiousness on the part of the ruler; careful husbanding of its resources, with at the same time a tender care for the interests of all classes; and the employing of the masses in the public service at suitable seasons.

"Let young people," said he, "show filial piety at home, respectfulness towards their elders when away from home; let them be circumspect, be truthful; their love going out freely towards all, cultivating good-will to men. And if, in such a walk, there be time or energy left for other things, let them employ it in the acquisition of literary or artistic accomplishments."

The disciple Tsz-hiš said, "The appreciation of worth in men of worth, thus diverting the mind from lascivious desires – ministering to parents while one is the most capable of so doing – serving one's ruler when one is able to devote himself entirely to that object – being sincere in one's language in intercourse with friends: this I certainly must call evidence of learning, though others may say there has been 'no learning.'"

Sayings of the Master: –

"If the great man be not grave, he will not be revered, neither can his learning be solid.

"Give prominent place to loyalty and sincerity.

"Have no associates in study who are not advanced somewhat like yourself.

"When you have erred, be not afraid to correct yourself."

A saying of the Scholar Tsang: –

"The virtue of the people is renewed and enriched when attention is seen to be paid to the departed, and the remembrance of distant ancestors kept and cherished."

Tsz-k'in put this query to his fellow disciple Tsz-kung: said he, "When our Master comes to this or that State, he learns without fail how it is being governed. Does he investigate matters? or are the facts given him?"

Tsz-kung answered, "Our Master is a man of pleasant manners, and of probity, courteous, moderate, and unassuming: it is by his being such that he arrives at the facts. Is not his way of arriving at things different from that of others?"

A saying of the Master: –

"He who, after three years' observation of the will of his father when alive, or of his past conduct if dead, does not deviate from that father's ways, is entitled to be called 'a dutiful son.'"

Sayings of the Scholar Yu: –

"For the practice of the Rules of Propriety,[1] one excellent way is to be natural. This naturalness became a great grace in the practice of kings of former times; let everyone, small or great, follow their example.

"It is not, however, always practicable; and it is not so in the case of a person who does things naturally, knowing that he should act so, and yet who neglects to regulate his acts according to the Rules.

"When truth and right are hand in hand, a statement will bear repetition. When respectfulness and propriety go hand in hand, disgrace and shame are kept afar-off. Remove all occasion for alienating those to whom you are bound by close ties, and you have them still to resort to."

A saying of the Master: –

---

[1] An important part of a Chinaman's education still. The text-book, "The Li Ki," contains rules for behavior and propriety for the whole life, from the cradle to the grave.

On Learning – Miscellaneous Sayings: –

"The man of greater mind who, when he is eating, craves not to eat to the full; who has a home, but craves not for comforts in it; who is active and earnest in his work and careful in his words; who makes towards men of high principle, and so maintains his own rectitude – that man may be styled a devoted student."

Tsz-kung asked, "What say you, sir, of the poor who do not cringe and fawn; and what of the rich who are without pride and haughtiness?" "They are passable," the Master replied; "yet they are scarcely in the same category as the poor who are happy, and the rich who love propriety."

"In the 'Book of the Odes,'" Tsz-kung went on to say, "we read of one

Polished, as by the knife and file,
The graving-tool, the smoothing-stone.

Does that coincide with your remark?"

"Ah! such as you," replied the Master,

"may well commence a discussion on the Odes. If one tell you how a thing goes, you know what ought to come."

"It does not greatly concern me," said the Master, "that men do not know me; my great concern is, my not knowing them."

BOOK TWO

Good Government – Filial Piety – The Superior Man

SAYINGS OF the Master: –

"Let a ruler base his government upon virtuous principles, and he will be like the pole-star, which remains steadfast in its place, while all the host of stars turn towards it.

"The 'Book of Odes' contains three

hundred pieces, but one expression in it may be taken as covering the purport of all, viz., Unswerving mindfulness.

"To govern simply by statute, and to reduce all to order by means of pains and penalties, is to render the people evasive, and devoid of any sense of shame.

"To govern upon principles of virtue, and to reduce them to order by the Rules of Propriety, would not only create in them the sense of shame, but would moreover reach them in all their errors.

"When I attained the age of fifteen, I became bent upon study. At thirty, I was a confirmed student. At forty, nought could move me from my course. At fifty, I comprehended the will and decrees of Heaven. At sixty, my ears were attuned to them. At seventy, I could follow my heart's desires, without overstepping the lines of rectitude."

To a question of Mang-i, as to what filial piety consisted in, the master replied, "In not being perverse." Afterwards, when Fan

Ch'i was driving him, the Master informed him of this question and answer, and Fan Ch'i asked, "What was your meaning?" The Master replied, "I meant that the Rules of Propriety should always be adhered to in regard to those who brought us into the world: in ministering to them while living, in burying them when dead, and afterwards in the offering to them of sacrificial gifts."

To a query of Mang Wu respecting filial piety, the Master replied, "Parents ought to bear but one trouble – that of their own sickness."

To a like question put by Tsz-yu, his reply was this: "The filial piety of the present day simply means the being able to support one's parents – which extends even to the case of dogs and horses, all of which may have something to give in the way of support. If there be no reverential feeling in the matter, what is there to distinguish between the cases?"

To a like question of Tsz-hia, he replied:

"The manner is the difficulty. If, in the case of work to be done, the younger folks simply take upon themselves the toil of it; or if, in the matter of meat and drink, they simply set these before their elders – is this to be taken as filial piety?"

Once the Master remarked, "I have conversed with Hwụi the whole day long, and he has controverted nothing that I have said, as if he were without wits. But when his back was turned, and I looked attentively at his conduct apart from me, I found it satisfactory in all its issues. No, indeed! Hwụi is not without his wits."

Other observations of the Master: –

"If you observe what things people (usually) take in hand, watch their motives, and note particularly what it is that gives them satisfaction, shall they be able to conceal from you what they are? Conceal themselves, indeed!

"Be versed in ancient lore, and familiarize yourself with the modern; then may you become teachers.

"The great man is not a mere receptacle."

In reply to Tsz-kung respecting the great man: –

"What he first says, as a result of his experience, he afterwards follows up.

"The great man is catholic-minded, and not one-sided. The common man is the reverse.

"Learning, without thought, is a snare; thought, without learning, is a danger.

"Where the mind is set much upon heterodox principles – there truly and indeed is harm."

To the disciple Tsz-lu the Master said, "Shall I give you a lesson about knowledge? When you know a thing, maintain that you know it; and when you do not, acknowledge your ignorance. This is characteristic of knowledge."

Tsz-chang was studying with an eye to official income. The Master addressed him thus: "Of the many things you hear hold aloof from those that are doubtful, and speak guardedly with reference to the rest; your mistakes will then be few. Also, of the many courses you see adopted, hold aloof from those that are risky, and carefully follow the others; you will then seldom have occasion for regret. Thus, being seldom mistaken in your utterances, and having few occasions for regret in the line you take, you are on the high road to your preferment."

To a question put to him by Duke Ngai[2] as to what should be done in order to render the people submissive to authority, Confucius replied, "Promote the straightforward, and reject those whose courses are crooked, and the thing will be effected. Promote the crooked and reject the straightforward, and the effect will be the reverse."

When Ki K'ang[3] asked of him how the people could be induced to show respect, loyalty, and willingness to be led, the Master

---

2 Of Lu (Confucius's native State).

3 Head of one of the "Three Families" of Lu.

answered, "Let there be grave dignity in him who has the oversight of them, and they will show him respect; let him be seen to be good to his own parents, and kindly in disposition, and they will be loyal to him; let him promote those who have ability, and see to the instruction of those who have it not, and they will be willing to be led."

Some one, speaking to Confucius, inquired, "Why, sir, are you not an administrator of government?" The Master rejoined, "What says the 'Book of the Annals,' with reference to filial duty? – 'Make it a point to be dutiful to your parents and amicable with your brethren; the same duties extend to an administrator.' If these, then, also make an administrator, how am I to take your words about being an administrator?"

On one occasion the Master remarked, "I know not what men are good for, on whose word no reliance can be placed. How should your carriages, large or little, get along without your whipple-trees or swing-trees?"

Tsz-chang asked if it were possible to forecast the state of the country ten generations hence. The Master replied in this manner: "The Yin dynasty adopted the rules and manners of the HiŠ line of kings, and it is possible to tell whether it retrograded or advanced. The Chow line has followed the Yin, adopting its ways, and whether there has been deterioration or improvement may also be determined. Some other line may take up in turn those of Chow; and supposing even this process to go on for a hundred generations, the result may be known."

Other sayings of the Master: –

"It is but flattery to make sacrificial offerings to departed spirits not belonging to one's own family.

"It is moral cowardice to leave undone what one perceives to be right to do."

BOOK THREE

Abuse of Proprieties in Ceremonial and Music

ALLUDING TO THE HEAD of the Ki family,[4] and the eight lines of posturers[5] before their

---

4 The Chief of the Ki clan was virtually the Duke of Lu, under whom Confucius for a time held office.

5 These posturers were mutes who took part in the ritual of the ancestral temple, waving

ancestral hall, Confucius remarked, "If the Ki can allow himself to go to this extent, to what extent will he not allow himself to go?"

The Three Families[6] were in the habit, during the Removal of the sacred vessels after sacrifice, of using the hymn commencing,

"Harmoniously the Princes
  Draw near with reverent tread,
Assisting in his worship
  Heaven's Son, the great and dread."

"How," exclaimed the Master, "can such

---

plumes, flags, etc. Each line or rank of these contained eight men. Only in the sovereign's household should there have been eight lines of them; a ducal family like the Ki should have had but six lines; a great official had four, and one of lower grade two. These were the gradations marking the status of families, and Confucius's sense of propriety was offended at the Ki's usurping in this way the appearance of royalty.

6 Three great families related to each other, in whose hands the government of the State of Lu then was, and of which the Ki was the chief.

words be appropriated in the ancestral hall of the Three Families?"

"Where a man," said he again, "has not the proper feelings due from one man to another, how will he stand as regards the Rules of Propriety? And in such a case, what shall we say of his sense of harmony?"

On a question being put to him by Lin Fang, a disciple, as to what was the radical idea upon which the Rules of Propriety were based, the Master exclaimed, "Ah! that is a large question. As to some rules, where there is likelihood of extravagance, they would rather demand economy; in those which relate to mourning, and where there is likelihood of being easily satisfied, what is wanted is real sorrow."

Speaking of the disorder of the times he remarked that while the barbarians on the North and East had their Chieftains, we here in this great country had nothing to compare with them in that respect: – we had lost these distinctions!

Alluding to the matter of the Chief of the Ki family worshipping on Tai-shan,[7] the Master said to Yen Yu, "Cannot you save him from this?" He replied, "It is beyond my power." "Alas, alas!" exclaimed the Master, "are we to say that the spirits of T'ai-shan have not as much discernment as Lin Fang?"

Of "the superior man," the Master observed, "In him there is no contentiousness. Say even that he does certainly contend with others, as in archery competitions; yet mark, in that case, how courteously he will bow and go up for the forfeit-cup, and come down again and give it to his competitor. In his very contest he is still the superior man."

Tsz-hiŠ once inquired what inference might be drawn from the lines –

"Dimples playing in witching smile,
Beautiful eyes, so dark, so bright!

---

[7] One of the five sacred mountains, worshipped upon only by the sovereign.

Oh, and her face may be thought the
while
Colored by art, red rose on white!"

"Coloring," replied the Master, "requires a pure and clear background." "Then," said the other, "rules of ceremony require to have a background!" "Ah!" exclaimed the Master, "you are the man to catch the drift of my thought. Such as you may well introduce a discussion on the Odes."

Said the Master, "As regards the ceremonial adopted and enforced by the HiŠ dynasty, I am able to describe it, although their own descendants in the State of Ki can adduce no adequate testimony in favor of its use there. So, too, I am able to describe the ceremonial of the Yin dynasty, although no more can the Sung people show sufficient reason for its continuance amongst themselves. And why cannot they do so? Because they have not documents enough, nor men learned enough. If only they had such, I could refer them to them in support of their usages.

"When I am present at the great quinquennial sacrifice to the **manes** of the royal ancestors," the Master said, "from the pouring-out of the oblation onwards, I have no heart to look on."

Some one asked what was the purport of this great sacrifice, and the Master replied, "I cannot tell. The position in the empire of him who could tell you is as evident as when you look at this" – pointing to the palm of his hand.

When he offered sacrifices to his ancestors, he used to act as if they were present before him. In offering to other spirits it was the same.

He would say, "If I do not myself take part in my offerings, it is all the same as if I did not offer them."

Wang-sun KiŠ asked him once, "What says the proverb, 'Better to court favor in the kitchen than in the drawing-room'?" The Master replied, "Nay, better say, He who has sinned against Heaven has none other to whom prayer may be addressed."

Of the Chow dynasty the Master remarked, "It looks back upon two other dynasties; and what a rich possession it has in its records of those times! I follow Chow!"

On his first entry into the grand temple, he inquired about every matter connected with its usages. Some one thereupon remarked, "Who says that the son of the man of Tsou[8] understands about ceremonial? On entering the grand temple he inquired about everything." This remark coming to the Master's ears, he said, "What I did is part of the ceremonial!"

"In archery," he said, "the great point to be observed is not simply the perforation of the leather; for men have not all the same strength. That was the fashion in the olden days."

Once, seeing that his disciple Tsz-kung was

---

8 Tsou was Confucius's birthplace; his father was governor of the town.

desirous that the ceremonial observance of offering a sheep at the new moon might be dispensed with, the Master said, "Ah! you grudge the loss of the sheep; I grudge the loss of the ceremony."

"To serve one's ruler nowadays," he remarked, "fully complying with the Rules of Propriety, is regarded by others as toadyism!"

When Duke Ting questioned him as to how a prince should deal with his ministers, and how they in turn should serve their prince, Confucius said in reply, "In dealing with his ministers a prince should observe the proprieties; in serving his prince a minister should observe the duty of loyalty."

Referring to the First of the Odes, he remarked that it was mirthful without being lewd, and sad also without being painful.

Duke Ngai asked the disciple Tsai Wo respecting the places for sacrificing to the Earth. The latter replied, "The Family of the Great Yu, of the HiŠ dynasty, chose a place of pine trees; the Yin founders chose cypresses; and the Chow founders chestnut trees, solemn and majestic, to inspire, 'tis said, the people with feelings of awe."

The Master on hearing of this exclaimed, "Never an allusion to things that have been enacted in the past! Never a remonstrance against what is now going on! He has gone away without a word of censure."

The Master once said of Kwan Chung, [9] "A small-minded man indeed!"

"Was he miserly?" some one asked.

"Miserly, indeed!" said he; "not that: he married three rimes, and he was not a man who restricted his official business to too few hands – how could he be miserly?"

---

[9] A renowned statesman who flourished about two hundred years before Confucius's time. A philosophical work on law and government, said to have been written by him, is still extant. He was regarded as a sage by the people, but he lacked, in Confucius's eyes, the one thing needful – propriety.

"He knew the Rules of Propriety, I suppose?"

"Judge: – Seeing that the feudal lords planted a screen at their gates, he too would have one at his! Seeing that when any two of the feudal lords met in friendly conclave they had an earthenware stand on which to place their inverted cups after drinking, he must have the same! If he knew the Rules of Propriety, who is there that does not know them?"

In a discourse to the Chief Preceptor of Music at the court of Lu, the Master said, "Music is an intelligible thing. When you begin a performance, let all the various instruments produce as it were one sound (inharmonious); then, as you go on, bring out the harmony fully, distinctly, and with uninterrupted flow, unto the end."

The warden of the border-town of I requested an interview with Confucius, and said, "When great men have come here, I have never yet failed to obtain a sight of them." The followers introduced him; and, on leaving, he said to them, "Sirs, why grieve at his loss of office? The empire has for long been without good government; and Heaven is about to use your master as its edict-announcer."

Comparing the music of the emperor Shun with the music of King Wu, the Master said, "That of Shun is beautiful throughout, and also good throughout. That of Wu is all of it beautiful, but scarcely all of it good."

"High station," said the Master, "occupied by men who have no large and generous heart; ceremonial performed with no reverence; duties of mourning engaging the attention, where there is absence of sorrow; – how should I look on, where this is the state of things?"

BOOK FOUR

Social Virtue – Superior and Inferior Man

SAYINGS OF THE MASTER: –

"It is social good feeling that gives charm to a neighborhood. And where is the wisdom of those who choose an abode where it does not abide?

"Those who are without it cannot abide long, either in straitened or in happy circumstances. Those who possess it find contentment in it. Those who are wise go after it as men go after gain.

"Only they in whom it exists can have right likings and dislikings for others.

"Where the will is set upon it, there will be no room for malpractices.

"Riches and honor are what men desire; but if they arrive at them by improper ways, they should not continue to hold them. Poverty and low estate are what men dislike; but if they arrive at such a condition by improper ways, they should not refuse it.

"If the 'superior man' make nought of social good feeling, how shall he fully bear that name?

"Not even whilst he eats his meal will the 'superior man' forget what he owes to his fellow-men. Even in hurried leave-takings, even in moments of frantic confusion, he keeps true to this virtue.

"I have not yet seen a lover of philanthropy, nor a hater of misanthropy – such, that the former did not take occasion to magnify that virtue in himself, and that the latter, in his positive practice of philanthropy, did not, at times, allow in his presence something savoring of misanthropy.

"Say you, is there any one who is able for one whole day to apply the energy of his mind to this virtue? Well, I have not seen any one whose energy was not equal to it. It may be there are such, but I have never met with them.

"The faults of individuals are peculiar to their particular class and surroundings; and it is by observing their faults that one comes to understand the condition of their good feelings towards their fellows.

"One may hear the right way in the morning, and at evening die.

"The scholar who is intent upon learning the right way, and who is yet ashamed of poor attire and poor food, is not worthy of being discoursed with.

"The masterly man's attitude to the world

is not exclusively this or that: whatsoever is right, to that he will be a party.

"The masterly man has an eye to virtue, the common man, to earthly things; the former has an eye to penalties for error – the latter, to favor.

"Where there is habitual going after gain, there is much ill-will.

"When there is ability in a ruler to govern a country by adhering to the Rules of Propriety, and by kindly condescension, what is wanted more? Where the ability to govern thus is wanting, what has such a ruler to do with the Rules of Propriety?

"One should not be greatly concerned at not being in office; but rather about the requirements in one's self for such a standing. Neither should one be so much concerned at being unknown; but rather with seeking to become worthy of being known."

Addressing his disciple Tsang Sin, the Master said, "Tsang Sin, the principles which

I inculcate have one main idea upon which they all hang." "Aye, surely," he replied.

When the Master was gone out the other disciples asked what was the purport of this remark. Tsang's answer was, "The principles of our Master's teaching are these – whole-heartedness and kindly forbearance; these and nothing more."

Other observations of the Master: –

"Men of loftier mind manifest themselves in their equitable dealings; small-minded men in their going after gain.

"When you meet with men of worth, think how you may attain to their level; when you see others of an opposite character, look within, and examine yourself.

"A son, in ministering to his parents, may (on occasion) offer gentle remonstrances; when he sees that their will is not to heed such, he should nevertheless still continue to show them reverent respect, never obstinacy; and if he have to suffer, let him do so without murmuring.

"Whilst the parents are still living, he should not wander far; or, if a wanderer, he should at least have some fixed address.

"If for three years he do not veer from the principles of his father, he may be called a dutiful son.

"A son should not ignore the years of his parents. On the one hand, they may be a matter for rejoicing (that they have been so many), and on the other, for apprehension (that so few remain).

"People in olden times were loth to speak out, fearing the disgrace of not being themselves as good as their words.

"Those who keep within restraints are seldom losers.

"To be slow to speak, but prompt to act, is the desire of the 'superior man.'

"Virtue dwells not alone: she must have neighbors."

An observation of Tsz-yu: – "Officiousness, in the service of princes, leads to disgrace: among friends, to estrangement."

BOOK FIVE

A Disciple and the Golden Rule – Miscellaneous

THE MASTER PRONOUNCED Kung-ye Ch'ang, a disciple, to be a marriageable person; for although lying bound in criminal fetters he had committed no crime. And he gave him his own daughter to wife.

Of Nan Yung, a disciple, he observed, that in a State where the government was well conducted he would not be passed over in its appointments, and in one where the government was ill conducted he would evade punishment and disgrace. And he caused his elder brother's daughter to be given in marriage to him.

Of Tsz-tsien, a disciple, he remarked, "A superior man indeed is the like of him! But had there been none of superior quality in Lu, how should this man have attained to this excellence?"

Tsz-kung asked, "What of me, then?" "You," replied the Master – "You are a receptacle." "Of what sort?" said he. "One for high and sacred use," was the answer.

Some one having observed of Yen Yung that he was good-natured towards others, but that he lacked the gift of ready speech, the Master said, "What need of that gift? To stand up before men and pour forth a stream of glib words is generally to make yourself obnoxious to them. I know not about his good-naturedness; but at any rate what need of that gift?"

When the Master proposed that Tsi-tiau K'ai should enter the government service, the latter replied, "I can scarcely credit it." The Master was gratified.

"Good principles are making no progress," once exclaimed the Master. "If I were to take a raft, and drift about on the sea, would Tsz-lu, I wonder, be my follower there?" That disciple was delighted at hearing the suggestion; whereupon the Master continued, "He surpasses me in his love of deeds of daring. But he does not in the least grasp the pith of my remark."

In reply to a question put to him by Mang Wu respecting Tsz-lu – as to whether he might be called good-natured towards others, the Master said, "I cannot tell"; but, on the question being put again, he answered, "Well, in an important State[10] he might be intrusted with the management of the military levies;

---

[10] Lit., a State of 1,000 war chariots.

but I cannot answer for his good nature."

"What say you then of Yen Yu?"

"As for Yen," he replied, "in a city of a thousand families, or in a secondary fief,[11] he might be charged with the governorship; but I cannot answer for his good-naturedness."

"Take Tsz-hwa, then; what of him?"

"Tsz-hwa," said he, "with a cincture girt upon him, standing as attendant at Court, might be charged with the addressing of visitors and guests; but as to his good-naturedness I cannot answer."

Addressing Tsz-kung, the Master said, "Which of the two is ahead of the other – yourself or Hwụi?" "How shall I dare," he replied, "even to look at Hwụi? Only let him hear one particular, and from that he knows ten; whereas I, if I hear one, may from it know two."

"You are not a match for him, I grant you," said the Master. "You are not his match."

---

11 Lit., a House of 100 war chariots.

Tsai Yu, a disciple, used to sleep in the daytime. Said the Master, "One may hardly carve rotten wood, or use a trowel to the wall of a manure-yard! In his case, what is the use of reprimand?

"My attitude towards a man in my first dealings with him," he added, "was to listen to his professions and to trust to his conduct. My attitude now is to listen to his professions, and to watch his conduct. My experience with Tsai Yu has led to this change.

"I have never seen," said the Master, "a man of inflexible firmness." Some one thereupon mentioned Shin Ch'ang, a disciple. "Ch'ang," said he, "is wanton; where do you get at his inflexibleness?"

Tsz-kung made the remark: "That which I do not wish others to put upon me, I also wish not to put upon others." "Nay," said the Master, "you have not got so far as that."

The same disciple once remarked, "There may be access so as to hear the Master's literary discourses, but when he is treating of human nature and the way of Heaven, there may not be such success."

Tsz-lu, after once hearing him upon some subject, and feeling himself as yet incompetent to carry into practice what he had heard, used to be apprehensive only lest he should hear the subject revived.

Tsz-kung asked how it was that Kung Wan had come to be so styled Wan (the talented). The Master's answer was, "Because, though a man of an active nature, he was yet fond of study, and he was not ashamed to stoop to put questions to his inferiors."

Respecting Tsz-ch'an,[12] the Master said that he had four of the essential qualities of the 'superior man': – in his own private walk he was humble-minded; in serving his superiors he was deferential; in his looking after the material welfare of the people he was generously kind; and in his exaction of

---

[12] A great statesman of Confucius's time.

public service from the latter he was just.

Speaking of Yen Ping, he said, "He was one who was happy in his mode of attaching men to him. However long the intercourse, he was always deferential to them."

Referring to Tsang Wan, he asked, "What is to be said of this man's discernment? – this man with his tortoise-house, with the pillar-heads and posts bedizened with scenes of hill and mere!"

Tsz-chang put a question relative to the chief Minister of Tsu, Tsz-wan. He said, "Three times he became chief Minister, and on none of these occasions did he betray any sign of exultation. Three times his ministry came to an end, and he showed no sign of chagrin. He used without fail to inform the new Minister as to the old mode of administration. What say you of him?"

"That he was a loyal man," said the Master.

"But was he a man of fellow-feeling?" said the disciple.

"Of that I am not sure," he answered; "how

am I to get at that?"

The disciple went on to say: – "After the assassination of the prince of Ts'i by the officer Ts'ui, the latter's fellow-official Ch'in Wan, who had half a score teams of horses, gave up all, and turned his back upon him. On coming to another State, he observed, 'There are here characters somewhat like that of our minister Ts'ui,' and he turned his back upon them. Proceeding to a certain other State, he had occasion to make the same remark, and left. What say you of him?"

"That he was a pure-minded man," answered the Master.

"But was he a man of fellow-feeling?" urged the disciple.

"Of that I am not sure," he replied; "how am I to get at that?"

Ki Wan was one who thought three times over a thing before he acted. The Master hearing this of him, observed, "Twice would have been enough."

Of Ning Wu, the Master said that when matters went well in the State he used to have his wits about him: but when they went wrong, he lost them. His intelligence might be equalled, but not his witlessness!

Once, when the Master lived in the State of Ch'in, he exclaimed, "Let me get home again! Let me get home! My school-children[13] are wild and impetuous! Though they are somewhat accomplished, and perfect in one sense in their attainments, yet they know not how to make nice discriminations."

Of Peh-I and Shuh Ts'i he said, "By the fact of their not remembering old grievances, they gradually did away with resentment."

Of Wei-shang Kau he said, "Who calls him straightforward? A person once begged some vinegar of him, and he begged it from a neighbor, and then presented him with it!"

"Fine speech," said he, "and studied mien,

---

[13] A familiar way of speaking of his disciples in their hearing.

and superfluous show of deference – of such things Tso-k'iu Ming was ashamed, I too am ashamed of such things. Also of hiding resentment felt towards an opponent and treating him as a friend – of this kind of thing he was ashamed, and so too am I."

Attended once by the two disciples Yen Yuen and Tsz-lu, he said, "Come now, why not tell me, each of you, what in your hearts you are really after?"

"I should like," said Tsz-lu, "for myself and my friends and associates, carriages and horses, and to be clad in light furs! nor would I mind much if they should become the worse for wear."

"And I should like," said Yen Yuen, "to live without boasting of my abilities, and without display of meritorious deeds."

Tsz-lu then said, "I should like, sir, to hear what your heart is set upon."

The Master replied, "It is this: – in regard to old people, to give them quiet and comfort; in regard to friends and associates, to be faithful to them; in regard to the young, to treat them with fostering affection and kindness."

On one occasion the Master exclaimed, "Ah, 'tis hopeless! I have not yet seen the man who can see his errors, so as inwardly to accuse himself."

"In a small cluster of houses there may well be," said he, "some whose integrity and sincerity may compare with mine; but I yield to none in point of love of learning."

BOOK SIX

More Characteristics – Wisdom – Philanthropy

OF YEN YUNG, a disciple, the Master said, "Yung might indeed do for a prince!"

On being asked by this Yen Yung his opinion of a certain individual, the Master replied, "He is passable. Impetuous, though."

"But," argued the disciple, "if a man habituate himself to a reverent regard for duty – even while in his way of doing things he is impetuous – in the oversight of the people committed to his charge, is he not passable? If, on the other hand, he habituate himself to impetuosity of mind, and show it also in his way of doing things, is he not then over-impetuous?"

"You are right," said the Master.

When the Duke Ngai inquired which of the disciples were devoted to learning, Confucius answered him, "There was one Yen Hwķi who loved it – a man whose angry feelings towards any particular person he did not suffer to visit upon another; a man who would never fall into the same error twice. Unfortunately his allotted time was short, and he died, and now his like is not to be found; I have never heard of one so devoted to learning."

While Tsz-hwa, a disciple, was away on a mission to Ts'i, the disciple Yen Yu, on behalf of his mother, applied for some grain. "Give her three pecks," said the Master. He applied for more. "Give her eight, then." Yen gave her fifty times that amount. The Master said, "When Tsz-hwa went on that journey to Ts'i, he had well-fed steeds yoked to his carriage, and was arrayed in light furs. I have learnt that the 'superior man' should help those whose needs are urgent, not help the rich to be more rich."

When Yuen Sz became prefect under him, he gave him nine hundred measures of grain, but the prefect declined to accept them.[14] "You must not," said the Master. "May they not be of use to the villages and hamlets around you?"

Speaking of Yen Yung again, the Master said, "If the offspring of a speckled ox be red in color, and horned, even though men may not wish to take it for sacrifice, would the

---

14 At this time Confucius was Criminal Judge in his native State of Lu. Yuen Sz had been a disciple. The commentators add that this was the officer's proper salary, and that he did wrong to refuse it.

spirits of the hills and streams reject it?"

Adverting to Hwķi again, he said, "For three months there would not be in his breast one thought recalcitrant against his feeling of good-will towards his fellow-men. The others may attain to this for a day or for a month, but there they end."

When asked by Ki K'ang whether Tsz-lu was fit to serve the government, the Master replied, "Tsz-lu is a man of decision: what should prevent him from serving the government?"

Asked the same question respecting Tsz-kung and Yen Yu he answered similarly, pronouncing Tsz-kung to be a man of perspicacity, and Yen Yu to be one versed in the polite arts.

When the head of the Ki family sent for Min Tsz-k'ien to make him governor of the town of Pi, that disciple said, "Politely decline for me. If the offer is renewed, then indeed I shall feel myself obliged to go and live on the further bank of the Wan."

Peh-niu had fallen ill, and the Master was inquiring after him. Taking hold of his hand held out from the window, he said, "It is taking him off! Alas, his appointed time has come! Such a man, and to have such an illness!"

Of Hwķi, again: "A right worthy man indeed was he! With his simple wooden dish of rice, and his one gourd-basin of drink, away in his poor back lane, in a condition too grievous for others to have endured, he never allowed his cheery spirits to droop. Aye, a right worthy soul was he!"

"It is not," Yen Yu once apologized, "that I do not take pleasure in your doctrines; it is that I am not strong enough." The Master rejoined, "It is when those who are not strong enough have made some moderate amount of progress that they fail and give up; but you are now drawing your own line for yourself."

Addressing Tsz-hiŠ, the Master said, "Let your scholarship be that of gentlemen, and not like that of common men."

When Tsz-yu became governor of Wu-shing, the Master said to him, "Do you find good men about you?" The reply was, "There is Tan-t'ai Mieh-ming, who when walking eschews by-paths, and who, unless there be some public function, never approaches my private residence."

"Mang Chi-fan," said the Master, "is no sounder of his own praises. During a stampede he was in the rear, and as they were about to enter the city gate he whipped up his horses, and said, 'Twas not my daring made me lag behind. My horses would not go.'"

Obiter dicta of the Master: –

"Whoever has not the glib utterance of the priest T'o, as well as the handsomeness of Prince ChŠu of Sung, will find it hard to keep out of harm's way in the present age.

"Who can go out but by that door? Why walks no one by these guiding principles?

"Where plain naturalness is more in

evidence than polish, we have – the man from the country. Where polish is more in evidence than naturalness, we have – the town scribe. It is when naturalness and polish are equally evident that we have the ideal man.

"The life of a man is – his rectitude. Life without it – such may you have the good fortune to avoid!

"They who know it are not as those who love it, nor they who love it as those who rejoice in it – that is, have the fruition of their love for it.

"To the average man, and those above the average, it is possible to discourse on higher subjects; to those from the average downwards, it is not possible."

Fan Ch'i put a query about wisdom. The Master replied, "To labor for the promoting of righteous conduct among the people of the land; to be serious in regard to spiritual beings, and to hold aloof from them; – this may be called wisdom."

To a further query, about philanthropy, he replied, "Those who possess that virtue find difficulty with it at first, success later.

"Men of practical knowledge," he said, "find their gratification among the rivers of the lowland, men of sympathetic social feeling find theirs among the hills. The former are active and bustling, the latter calm and quiet. The former take their day of pleasure, the latter look to length of days."

Alluding to the States of Ts'i and Lu, he observed, that Ts'i, by one change, might attain to the condition of Lu; and that Lu, by one change, might attain to good government.

An exclamation of the Master (satirizing the times, when old terms relating to government were still used while bereft of their old meaning): – "A quart, and not a quart! **quart**, indeed! **quart**, indeed!"

Tsai Wo, a disciple, put a query. Said he, "Suppose a philanthropic person were told, 'There's a fellow-creature down in the well!'

Would he go down after him?"

"Why should he really do so?" answered the Master. "The good man or, a superior man might be induced to go, but not to go down. He may be misled, but not befooled."

"The superior man," said he, "with his wide study of books, and hedging himself round by the Rules of Propriety, is not surely, after all that, capable of overstepping his bounds."

Once when the Master had had an interview with Nan-tsz, which had scandalized his disciple Tsz-lu, he uttered the solemn adjuration, "If I have done aught amiss, may Heaven reject me! may Heaven reject me!"

"How far-reaching," said he, "is the moral excellence that flows from the Constant Mean![15] It has for a long time been rare among the people."

---

15 The doctrine afterwards known by that name, and which gave its title to a Confucian treatise.

Tsz-kung said, "Suppose the case of one who confers benefits far and wide upon the people, and who can, in so doing, make his bounty universally felt – how would you speak of him? Might he be called philanthropic?"

The Master exclaimed, "What a work for philanthropy! He would require indeed to be a sage! He would put into shade even Yau and Shun! – Well, a philanthropic person, desiring for himself a firm footing, is led on to give one to others; desiring for himself an enlightened perception of things, he is led on to help others to be similarly enlightened. If one could take an illustration coming closer home to us than yours, that might be made the starting-point for speaking about philanthropy."

BOOK SEVEN

Characteristics of Confucius – An Incident

SAID THE MASTER: –

"I, as a transmitter[16] and not an originator, and as one who believes in and loves the ancients, venture to compare myself with our old P'ang.

---

16 In reference to his editing the six Classics of his time.

"What find you indeed in me? – a quiet brooder and memorizer; a student never satiated with learning; an unwearied monitor of others!

"The things which weigh heavily upon my mind are these – failure to improve in the virtues, failure in discussion of what is learnt, inability to walk according to knowledge received as to what is right and just, inability also to reform what has been amiss."

In his hours of recreation and refreshment the Master's manner was easy and unconstrained, affable and winning.

Once he exclaimed, "Alas! I must be getting very feeble; 'tis long since I have had a repetition of the dreams in which I used to see the Duke of Chow.[17]

---

[17] This was one of his "beloved ancients," famous for what he did in helping to found the dynasty of Chow, a man of great political wisdom, a scholar also, and poet. It was the "dream" of Confucius's life to restore the country to the condition in which the Duke of Chow left it.

"Concentrate the mind," said he, "upon the Good Way.

"Maintain firm hold upon Virtue.

"Rely upon Philanthropy.

"Find recreation in the Arts.[18]

"I have never withheld instruction from any, even from those who have come for it with the smallest offering.

"No subject do I broach, however, to those who have no eager desire to learn; no encouraging hint do I give to those who show no anxiety to speak out their ideas; nor have I anything more to say to those who, after I have made clear one corner of the subject, cannot from that give me the other three."

If the Master was taking a meal, and there were any in mourning beside him, he would not eat to the full.

On one day on which he had wept, on that

---

18 These were six in number, viz.: Ceremonial, Music, Archery, Horsemanship, Language, and Calculation.

day he would not sing.

Addressing his favorite disciple, he said, "To you only and myself it has been given to do this – to go when called to serve, and to go back into quiet retirement when released from office."

Tsz-lu, hearing the remark said, "But if, sir, you had the handling of the army of one of the greater States,[19] whom would you have associated with you in that case?"

The Master answered: –

"Not the one 'who'll rouse the tiger,'
Not the one 'who'll wade the Ho;'

not the man who can die with no regret. He must be one who should watch over affairs with apprehensive caution, a man fond of strategy, and of perfect skill and effectiveness in it."

---

[19] Lit., three forces. Each force consisted of 12,500 men, and three of such forces were the equipment of a greater State.

As to wealth, he remarked, "If wealth were an object that I could go in quest of, I should do so even if I had to take a whip and do grooms' work. But seeing that it is not, I go after those objects for which I have a liking."

Among matters over which he exercised great caution were times of fasting, war, and sickness.

When he was in the State of Ts'i, and had heard the ancient Shau music, he lost all perception of the taste of his meat. "I had no idea," said he, "that music could have been brought to this pitch."

In the course of conversation Yen Yu said, "Does the Master take the part of the Prince of Wei?" "Ah yes!" said Tsz-kung, "I will go and ask him that."

On going in to him, that disciple began, "What sort of men were Peh-I and Shuh Ts'i?" "Worthies of the olden time," the Master replied. "Had they any feelings of resentment?" was the next question. "Their aim and object," he answered, "was that of doing the duty which every man owes to his fellows, and they succeeded in doing it; – what room further for feelings of resentment?" The questioner on coming out said, "The Master does not take his part."

"With a meal of coarse rice," said the Master, "and with water to drink, and my bent arm for my pillow – even thus I can find happiness. Riches and honors without righteousness are to me as fleeting clouds."

"Give me several years more to live," said he, "and after fifty years' study of the 'Book of Changes' I might come to be free from serious error."

The Master's regular subjects of discourse were the "Books of the Odes" and "History," and the up-keeping of the Rules of Propriety. On all of these he regularly discoursed.

The Duke of Shih questioned Tsz-lu about Confucius, and the latter did not answer.

Hearing of this, the Master said, "Why did you not say, He is a man with a mind so intent on his pursuits that he forgets his food, and finds such pleasure in them that he forgets his troubles, and does not know that old age is coming upon him?"

"As I came not into life with any knowledge of it," he said, "and as my likings are for what is old, I busy myself in seeking knowledge there."

Strange occurrences, exploits of strength, deeds of lawlessness, references to spiritual beings – such-like matters the Master avoided in conversation.

"Let there," he said, "be three men walking together: from that number I should be sure to find my instructors; for what is good in them I should choose out and follow, and what is not good I should modify."

On one occasion he exclaimed, "Heaven begat Virtue in me; what can man do unto me?"

To his disciples he once said, "Do you look upon me, my sons, as keeping anything secret from you? I hide nothing from you. I do nothing that is not manifest to your eyes, my disciples. That is so with me."

Four things there were which he kept in view in his teaching – scholarliness, conduct of life, honesty, faithfulness.

"It is not given to me," he said, "to meet with a sage; let me but behold a man of superior mind, and that will suffice. Neither is it given to me to meet with a good man; let me but see a man of constancy, and it will suffice. It is difficult for persons to have constancy, when they pretend to have that which they are destitute of, to be full when they are empty, to do things on a grand scale when their means are contracted!"

When the Master fished with hook and line, he did not also use a net. When out with his bow, he would never shoot at game in cover.

"Some there may be," said he, "who do things in ignorance of what they do. I am not of these. There is an alternative way of knowing things, viz. – to sift out the good from the many things one hears, and follow it; and to keep in memory the many things one sees."

Pupils from Hu-hiang were difficult to speak with. One youth came to interview the Master, and the disciples were in doubt whether he ought to have been seen. "Why so much ado," said the Master, "at my merely permitting his approach, and not rather at my allowing him to draw back? If a man have cleansed himself in order to come and see me, I receive him as such; but I do not undertake for what he will do when he goes away."

"Is the philanthropic spirit far to seek, indeed?" the Master exclaimed; "I wish for it, and it is with me!"

The Minister of Crime in the State of Ch'in asked Confucius whether Duke Ch'an, of Lu was acquainted with the Proprieties; and he answered, "Yes, he knows them."

When Confucius had withdrawn, the minister bowed to Wu-ma K'i, a disciple, and motioned to him to come forward. He said, "I have heard that superior men show no partiality; are they, too, then, partial? That prince took for his wife a lady of the Wu family, having the same surname as himself, and had her named 'Lady Tsz of Wu, the elder,' If he knows the Proprieties, then who does not?"

The disciple reported this to the Master, who thereupon remarked, "Well for me! If I err in any way, others are sure to know of it."

When the Master was in company with any one who sang, and who sang well, he must needs have the song over again, and after that would join in it.

"Although in letters," he said, "I may have none to compare with me, yet in my personification of the 'superior man' I have not as yet been successful."

"'A Sage and a Philanthropist?' How should I have the ambition?" said he. "All that I can well be called is this – An insatiable student, an unwearied teacher; – this, and no more."

– "Exactly what we, your disciples, cannot by any learning manage to be," said Kung-si Hwa.

Once when the Master was seriously ill, Tsz-lu requested to be allowed to say prayers for him. "Are such available?" asked the Master. "Yes," said he; "and the Manual of Prayers says, 'Pray to the spirits above and to those here below,'"

"My praying has been going on a long while," said the Master.

"Lavish living," he said, "renders men disorderly; miserliness makes them hard. Better, however, the hard than the disorderly."

Again, "The man of superior mind is placidly composed; the small-minded man is in a constant state of perturbation."

The Master was gentle, yet could be severe; had an over-awing presence, yet was not violent; was deferential, yet easy.

BOOK EIGHT

Sayings of Tsang – Sentences of the Master

SPEAKING OF T'AI-PIH the Master said that he might be pronounced a man of the highest moral excellence; for he allowed the empire to pass by him onwards to a third heir; while the people, in their ignorance of his motives, were unable to admire him for so doing.

"Without the Proprieties," said the Master, "we have these results: for deferential demeanor, a worried one; for calm attentiveness, awkward bashfulness; for manly conduct, disorderliness; for straightforwardness, perversity.

"When men of rank show genuine care for those nearest to them in blood, the people rise to the duty of neighborliness and sociability. And when old friendships among them are not allowed to fall off, there will be a cessation of underhand practices among the people."

The Scholar Tsang was once unwell, and calling his pupils to him he said to them, "Disclose to view my feet and my hands. What says the Ode? –

'Act as from a sense of danger,
With precaution and with care,
As a yawning gulf o'erlooking,
As on ice that scarce will bear,'

At all times, my children, I know how to keep myself free from bodily harm."

Again, during an illness of his, Mang King, an official, went to ask after him. The Scholar had some conversation with him, in the course of which he said –

"'Doleful the cries of a dying bird,
Good the last words of a dying man,'

There are three points which a man of rank in the management of his duties should set store upon: – A lively manner and deportment, banishing both severity and laxity; a frank and open expression of countenance, allied closely with sincerity; and a tone in his utterances utterly free from any approach to vulgarity and impropriety. As to matters of bowls and dishes, leave such things to those who are charged with the care of them."

Another saying of the Scholar Tsang: "I once had a friend who, though he possessed ability, would go questioning men of none, and, though surrounded by numbers, would go with his questions to isolated individuals; who also, whatever he might have, appeared as if he were without it, and, with all his substantial acquirements, made as though his mind were a mere blank; and when insulted would not retaliate; – this was ever his way."

Again he said: "The man that is capable of being intrusted with the charge of a minor on the throne, and given authority over a large territory, and who, during the important term of his superintendence cannot be forced out of his position, is not such a 'superior man'? That he is, indeed."

Again: – "The learned official must not be without breadth and power of endurance: the burden is heavy, and the way is long.

"Suppose that he take his duty to his fellow-men as his peculiar burden, is that not indeed a heavy one? And since only with death it is done with, is not the way long?"

Sentences of the Master: –

"From the 'Book of Odes' we receive impulses; from the 'Book of the Rules,' stability; from the 'Book on Music,' refinement.[20]

"The people may be put into the way they should go, though they may not be put into the way of understanding it.

"The man who likes bravery, and yet groans under poverty, has mischief in him. So, too, has the misanthrope, groaning at any severity shown towards him.

"Even if a person were adorned with the gifts of the Duke of Chow, yet if he were proud and avaricious, all the rest of his qualities would not indeed be worth looking at.

"Not easily found is the man who, after three years' study, has failed to come upon some fruit of his toil.

---

[20] Comparison of three of the Classics: the "Shi-King," the "Li Ki," and the "Yoh." The last is lost.

"The really faithful lover of learning holds fast to the Good Way till death.

"He will not go into a State in which a downfall is imminent, nor take up his abode in one where disorder reigns. When the empire is well ordered he will show himself; when not, he will hide himself away. Under a good government it will be a disgrace to him if he remain in poverty and low estate; under a bad one, it would be equally disgraceful to him to hold riches and honors.

"If not occupying the office, devise not the policy.

"When the professor Chi began his duties, how grand the finale of the First of the Odes used to be! How it rang in one's ears!

"I cannot understand persons who are enthusiastic and yet not straightforward; nor those who are ignorant and yet not attentive; nor again those folks who are simple-minded and yet untrue.

"Learn, as if never overtaking your object, and yet as if apprehensive of losing it.

"How sublime was the handling of the empire by Shun and Yu! – it was as nothing to them!

"How great was Yau as a prince! Was he not sublime! Say that Heaven only is great, then was Yau alone after its pattern! How profound was he! The people could not find a name for him. How sublime in his achievements! How brilliant in his scholarly productions!"

Shun had for his ministers five men, by whom he ordered the empire.

King Wu (in his day) stated that he had ten men as assistants for the promotion of order.

With reference to these facts Confucius observed, "Ability is hard to find. Is it not so indeed? During the three years' interregnum between Yau and Shun there was more of it than in the interval before this present dynasty appeared. There were, at this latter period, one woman, and nine men only.

"When two-thirds of the empire were held by King Wan, he served with that portion the House of Yin. We speak of the virtue of the House of Chow; we may say, indeed, that it reached the pinnacle of excellence."

"As to Yu," added the Master, "I can find no flaw in him. Living on meagre food and drink; yet providing to the utmost in his filial offerings to the spirits of the dead! Dressing in coarse garments; yet most elegant when vested in his sacrificial apron and coronet! Dwelling in a poor palace; yet exhausting his energies over those boundary-ditches and watercourses! I can find no flaw in Yu."

BOOK NINE

His Favorite Disciple's Opinion of Him

TOPICS ON WHICH the Master rarely spoke were – Advantage, and Destiny, and Duty of man to man.

A man of the village of Tah-hiang exclaimed of him, "A great man is Confucius! – a man of extensive learning, and yet in nothing has he quite made himself a name!"

The Master heard of this, and mentioning it to his disciples he said, "What then shall I take in hand? Shall I become a carriage driver, or an archer? Let me be a driver!"

"The sacrificial cap," he once said, "should, according to the Rules, be of linen; but in these days it is of pure silk. However, as it is economical, I do as all do.

"The Rule says, 'Make your bow when at the lower end of the hall'; but nowadays the bowing is done at the upper part. This is great freedom; and I, though I go in opposition to the crowd, bow when at the lower end."

The Master barred four words: – he would have no "shall's," no "must's," no "certainty's," no "I's."

Once, in the town of K'wang fearing that his life was going to be taken, the Master exclaimed, "King Wan is dead and gone; but is not '**wan**'[21] with you here? If Heaven

---

21 "Wan" was the honorary appellation of the great sage and ruler, whose praise is in the

be about to allow this '**wan**' to perish, then they who survive its decease will get no benefit from it. But so long as Heaven does not allow it to perish, what can the men of K'wang do to me?"

A high State official, after questioning Tsz-kung, said, "Your Master is a sage, then? How many and what varied abilities must be his!"

The disciple replied, "Certainly Heaven is allowing him full opportunities of becoming a sage, in addition to the fact that his abilities are many and varied."

When the Master heard of this he remarked, "Does that high official know me? In my early

---

"Shi-King" as one of the founders of the Chow dynasty, and the term represented civic talent and virtues, as distinct from Wu, the martial talent – the latter being the honorary title of his son and successor. "Wan" also often stands for literature and polite accomplishments. Here Confucius simply means, "If you kill me, you kill a sage."

years my position in life was low, and hence my ability in many ways, though exercised in trifling matters. In the gentleman is there indeed such variety of ability? No."

From this, the disciple Lau used to say, "'Twas a saying of the Master: 'At a time when I was not called upon to use them, I acquired my proficiency in the polite arts.'"

"Am I, indeed," said the Master, "possessed of knowledge? I know nothing. Let a vulgar fellow come to me with a question – a man with an emptyish head – I may thrash out with him the matter from end to end, and exhaust myself in doing it!"

"Ah!" exclaimed he once, "the phoenix does not come! and no symbols issue from the river! May I not as well give up?"

Whenever the Master met with a person in mourning, or with one in full-dress cap and kirtle, or with a blind person, although they might be young persons, he would make a point of rising on their appearance, or, if crossing their path, would do so with quickened step!

Once Yen Yuen exclaimed with a sigh (with reference to the Master's doctrines), "If I look up to them, they are ever the higher; if I try to penetrate them, they are ever the harder; if I gaze at them as if before my eyes, lo, they are behind me! – Gradually and gently the Master with skill lures men on. By literary lore he gave me breadth; by the Rules of Propriety he narrowed me down. When I desire a respite, I find it impossible; and after I have exhausted my powers, there seems to be something standing straight up in front of me, and though I have the mind to make towards it I make no advance at all."

Once when the Master was seriously ill, Tsz-lu induced the other disciples to feign they were high officials acting in his service. During a respite from his malady the Master exclaimed, "Ah! how long has Tsz-lu's conduct been false? Whom should I delude, if I were to pretend to have officials under me, having none? Should I deceive

Heaven? Besides, were I to die, I would rather die in the hands of yourselves, my disciples, than in the hands of officials. And though I should fail to have a grand funeral over me, I should hardly be left on my death on the public highway, should I?"

Tsz-kung once said to him, "Here is a fine gem. Would you guard it carefully in a casket and store it away, or seek a good price for it and sell it?" "Sell it, indeed," said the Master – "that would I; but I should wait for the bidder."

The Master protested he would "go and live among the nine wild tribes."

"A rude life," said some one; – "how could you put up with it?"

"What rudeness would there be," he replied, "if a 'superior man' was living in their midst?"

Once he remarked, "After I came back from Wei to Lu the music was put right, and each of the Festal Odes and Hymns was given its appropriate place and use."

"Ah! which one of these following," he asked on one occasion, "are to be found exemplified in me – proper service rendered to superiors when abroad; duty to father and elder brother when at home; duty that shrinks from no exertion when dear ones die; and keeping free from the confusing effects of wine?"

Standing once on the bank of a mountain stream, he said (musingly), "Like this are those that pass away – no cessation, day or night!"

Other sayings: –

"Take an illustration from the making of a hill. A simple basketful is wanting to complete it, and the work stops. So I stop short.

"Take an illustration from the levelling of the ground. Suppose again just one basketful is left, when the work has so progressed. There I desist!

"Ah! it was Hwꞔi, was it not? who, when I had given him his lesson, was the unflagging one!

"Alas for Hwķi! I saw him ever making progress. I never saw him stopping short.

"Blade, but no bloom – or else bloom, but no produce; aye, that is the way with some!

"Reverent regard is due to youth. How know we what difference there may be in them in the future from what they are now? Yet when they have reached the age of forty or fifty, and are still unknown in the world, then indeed they are no more worthy of such regard.

"Can any do otherwise than assent to words said to them by way of correction? Only let them reform by such advice, and it will then be reckoned valuable. Can any be other than pleased with words of gentle suasion? Only let them comply with them fully, and such also will be accounted valuable. With those who are pleased without so complying, and those who assent but do not reform, I can do nothing at all.

"Give prominent place to loyalty and sincerity.

"Have no associates in study who are not advanced somewhat like yourself.

"When you have erred, be not afraid to correct yourself.

"It may be possible to seize and carry off the chief commander of a large army, but not possible so to rob one poor fellow of his will.

"One who stands – clad in hempen robe, the worse for wear – among others clad in furs of fox and badger, and yet unabashed – 'tis Tsz-lu, that, is it not?"

Tsz-lu used always to be humming over the lines –

"From envy and enmity free,
What deed doth he other than good?"

"How should such a rule of life," asked the Master, "be sufficient to make any one good?"

"When the year grows chilly, we know the pine and cypress are the last to fade.

"The wise escape doubt; the good-hearted, trouble; the bold, apprehension.

"Some may study side by side, and yet be asunder when they come to the logic of things. Some may go on together in this latter course, but be wide apart in the standards they reach in it. Some, again, may together reach the same standard, and yet be diverse in weight of character."

"The blossom is out on the cherry tree,
With a flutter on every spray.
Dost think that my thoughts go not out
  to thee?
Ah, why art thou far away!"

Commenting on these lines the Master said, "There can hardly have been much 'thought going out,' What does distance signify?"

BOOK TEN

Confucius in Private and Official Life

IN HIS OWN VILLAGE, Confucius presented a somewhat plain and simple appearance, and looked unlike a man who possessed ability of speech.

But in the ancestral temple, and at Court, he spoke with the fluency and accuracy of a debater, but ever guardedly.

At Court, conversing with the lower order of great officials, he spoke somewhat firmly and directly; with those of the higher order his tone was somewhat more affable.

When the prince was present he was constrainedly reverent in his movements, and showed a proper degree of grave dignity in demeanor.

Whenever the prince summoned him to act as usher to the Court, his look would change somewhat, and he would make as though he were turning round to do obeisance.

He would salute those among whom he took up his position, using the right hand or the left, and holding the skirts of his robe in proper position before and behind. He would make his approaches with quick step, and with elbows evenly bent outwards.

When the visitor withdrew, he would not fail to report the execution of his commands, with the words, "The visitor no longer looks back."

When he entered the palace gate, it was

with the body somewhat bent forward, almost as though he could not be admitted. When he stood still, this would never happen in the middle of the gateway; nor when moving about would he ever tread on the threshold. When passing the throne, his look would change somewhat, he would turn aside and make a sort of obeisance, and the words he spoke seemed as though he were deficient in utterance.

On going up the steps to the audience chamber, he would gather up with both hands the ends of his robe, and walk with his body bent somewhat forward, holding back his breath like one in whom respiration has ceased. On coming out, after descending one step his countenance would relax and assume an appearance of satisfaction. Arrived at the bottom, he would go forward with quick step, his elbows evenly bent outwards, back to his position, constrainedly reverent in every movement.

When holding the sceptre in his hand, his

body would be somewhat bent forward, as if he were not equal to carrying it; wielding it now higher, as in a salutation, now lower, as in the presentation of a gift; his look would also be changed and appear awestruck; and his gait would seem retarded, as if he were obeying some restraining hand behind.

When he presented the gifts of ceremony, he would assume a placid expression of countenance. At the private interview he would be cordial and affable.

The good man would use no purple or violet colors for the facings of his dress.[22] Nor would he have red or orange color for his undress.[23] For the hot season he wore a singlet, of either coarse or fine texture, but would also feel bound to have an outer

---

22 Because, it is said, such colors were adopted in fasting and mourning.

23 Because they did not belong to the five correct colors (viz. green, yellow, carnation, white, and black), and were affected more by females.

garment covering it. For his black robe he had lamb's wool; for his white one, fawn's fur; and for his yellow one, fox fur. His furred undress robe was longer, but the right sleeve was shortened. He would needs have his sleeping-dress one and a half times his own length. For ordinary home wear he used thick substantial fox or badger furs. When he left off mourning, he would wear all his girdle trinkets. His kirtle in front, when it was not needed for full cover, he must needs have cut down. He would never wear his (black) lamb's-wool, or a dark-colored cap, when he went on visits of condolence to mourners.[24] On the first day of the new moon, he must have on his Court dress and to Court. When observing his fasts, he made a point of having bright, shiny garments, made of linen. He must also at such times vary his food, and move his seat to another part of his dwelling-room.

---

[24] Since white was, as it is still, the mourning color.

As to his food, he never tired of rice so long as it was clean and pure, nor of hashed meats when finely minced. Rice spoiled by damp, and sour, he would not touch, nor tainted fish, nor bad meat, nor aught of a bad color or smell, nor aught overdone in cooking, nor aught out of season. Neither would he eat anything that was not properly cut, or that lacked its proper seasonings. Although there might be an abundance of meat before him, he would not allow a preponderance of it to rob the rice of its beneficial effect in nutrition. Only in the matter of wine did he set himself no limit, yet he never drank so much as to confuse himself. Tradesmen's wines, and dried meats from the market, he would not touch. Ginger he would never have removed from the table during a meal. He was not a great eater. Meat from the sacrifices at the prince's temple he would never put aside till the following day. The meat of his own offerings he would never give out after three days' keeping, for after that time none were to eat it.

At his meals he would not enter into discussions; and when reposing (afterwards) he would not utter a word.

Even should his meal consist only of coarse rice and vegetable broth or melons, he would make an offering, and never fail to do so religiously.

He would never sit on a mat that was not straight.

After a feast among his villagers, he would wait before going away until the old men had left.

When the village people were exorcising the pests, he would put on his Court robes and stand on the steps of his hall to receive them.

When he was sending a message of inquiry to a person in another State, he would bow twice on seeing the messenger off.

Ki K'ang once sent him a present of some medicine. He bowed, and received it; but remarked, "Until I am quite sure of its properties I must not venture to taste it."

Once when the stabling was destroyed by fire, he withdrew from the Court, and asked, "Is any person injured? " – without inquiring as to the horses.

Whenever the prince sent him a present of food, he was particular to set his mat in proper order, and would be the first one to taste it. If the prince's present was one of raw meat, he must needs have it cooked, and make an oblation of it. If the gift were a live animal, he would be sure to keep it and care for it.

When he was in waiting, and at a meal with the prince, the prince would make the offering,[25] and he (the Master) was the pregustator.

When unwell, and the prince came to see him, he would arrange his position so that his head inclined towards the east, would put over him his Court robes, and draw his

---

[25] The act of "grace," before eating.

girdle across them.

When summoned by order of the prince, he would start off without waiting for his horses to be put to.

On his entry into the Grand Temple, he inquired about everything connected with its usages.

If a friend died, and there were no near relatives to take him to, he would say, “Let him be buried from my house.”

For a friend’s gift – unless it consisted of meat that had been offered in sacrifice – he would not bow, even if it were a carriage and horses.

In repose he did not lie like one dead. In his home life he was not formal in his manner.

Whenever he met with a person in mourning, even though it were a familiar acquaintance, he would be certain to change his manner; and when he met with any one in full-dress cap, or with any blind person, he would also unfailingly put on a different look, even though he were himself in undress at the time.

In saluting any person wearing mourning he would bow forwards towards the front bar of his carriage; in the same manner he would also salute the bearer of a census-register.

When a sumptuous banquet was spread before him, a different expression would be sure to appear in his features, and he would rise up from his seat.

At a sudden thunder-clap, or when the wind grew furious, his look would also invariably be changed.

On getting into his car, he would never fail (first) to stand up erect, holding on by the strap. When in the car, he would never look about, nor speak hastily, nor bring one hand to the other.

"Let one but make a movement in his
face,
And the bird will rise and seek some
safer place."

Apropos of this, he said, “Here is a hen-pheasant from Shan Liang – and in season! and in season!” After Tsz-lu had got it prepared, he smelt it thrice, and then rose up from his seat.

BOOK ELEVEN

Comparative Worth of His Disciples

"THE FIRST TO MAKE progress in the Proprieties and in Music," said the Master, "are plain countrymen; after them, the men of higher standing. If I had to employ any of them, I should stand by the former."

"Of those," said he, "who were about me when I was in the Ch'in and Ts'ai States, not one now is left to approach my door."

"As for Hwui,"[26] said the Master, "he is not one to help me on: there is nothing I say but he is not well satisfied with."

"What a dutiful son was Min Tsz-k'ien!" he exclaimed. "No one finds occasion to differ from what his parents and brothers have said of him."

Nan Yung used to repeat three times over the lines in the Odes about the white sceptre. Confucius caused his own elder brother's daughter to be given in marriage to him.

When Ki K'ang inquired which of the disciples were fond of learning, Confucius answered him, "There was one Yen Hwụi who was fond of it; but unfortunately his

---

[26] The men of virtuous life were Yen Yuen (Hwụi), Min Tsz-k'ien, Yen Pihniu, and Chung-kung (Yen Yung); the speakers and debaters were Tsai Wo and Tsz-kung; the (capable) government servants were Yen Yu and Tsz-lu; the literary students, Tsz-yu and Tsz-hiŠ.

allotted time was short, and he died; and now his like is not to be found."

When Yen Yuen died, his father, Yen Lu, begged for the Master's carriage in order to get a shell for his coffin. "Ability or no ability," said the Master, "every father still speaks of 'my son.' When my own son Li died, and the coffin for him had no shell to it, I know I did not go on foot to get him one; but that was because I was, though retired, in the wake of the ministers, and could not therefore well do so."

On the death of Yen Yuen the Master exclaimed, "Ah me! Heaven is ruining me, Heaven is ruining me!"

On the same occasion, his wailing for that disciple becoming excessive, those who were about him said, "Sir, this is too much!" – "Too much?" said he; "if I am not to do so for him, then – for whom else?"

The disciples then wished for the deceased a grand funeral. The Master could not on his part consent to this. They nevertheless gave him one. Upon this he remarked, "He used to look upon me as if I were his father. I could never, however, look on him as a son. Twas not my mistake, but yours, my children."

Tsz-lu propounded a question about ministering to the spirits of the departed. The Master replied, "Where there is scarcely the ability to minister to living men, how shall there be ability to minister to the spirits?" On his venturing to put a question concerning death, he answered, "Where there is scarcely any knowledge about life, how shall there be any about death?"

The disciple Min was by his side, looking affable and bland; Tsz-lu also, looking careless and intrepid; and Yen Yu and Tsz-kung, firm and precise. The Master was cheery. "One like Tsz-lu there," said he, "does not come to a natural end."

Some persons in Lu were taking measures in regard to the Long Treasury House. Min Tsz-k'ien observed, "How if it were repaired on the old lines?" The Master upon this remarked, "This fellow is not a talker, but when he does speak he is bound to hit the mark!"

"There is Yu's harpsichord," exclaimed the Master – "what is it doing at my door?" On seeing, however, some disrespect shown to him by the other disciples, he added, "Yu has got as far as the top of the hall; only he has not yet entered the house."

Tsz-kung asked which was the worthier of the two – Tsz-chang or Tsz-hiŠ. "The former," answered the Master, "goes beyond the mark; the latter falls short of it."

"So then Tsz-chang is the better of the two, is he?" said he.

"To go too far," he replied, "is about the same as to fall short."

The Chief of the Ki family was a wealthier man than the Duke of Chow had been, and yet Yen Yu gathered and hoarded for him, increasing his wealth more and more.

"He is no follower of mine," said the Master.

"It would serve him right, my children, to sound the drum, and set upon him."

Characteristics of four disciples: – Tsz-kŠu was simple-minded; Tsang Si, a dullard; Tsz-chang, full of airs; Tsz-lu, rough.

"As to Hwḳi," said the Master, "he comes near to perfection, while frequently in great want. Tsz-kung does not submit to the appointments of Heaven; and yet his goods are increased; – he is often successful in his calculations."

Tsz-chang wanted to know some marks of the naturally Good Man.

"He does not walk in others' footprints," said the Master; "yet he does not get beyond the hall into the house."

Once the Master said, "Because we allow that a man's words have something genuine in them, are they necessarily those of a superior man? or words carrying only an outward semblance and show of gravity?"

Tsz-lu put a question about the practice of precepts one has heard. The Master's reply was, “In a case where there is a father or elder brother still left with you, how should you practise all you hear?”

When, however, the same question was put to him by Yen Yu, his reply was, “Yes; do so.”

Kung-si Hwa animadverted upon this to the Master. “Tsz-lu asked you, sir,” said he, “about the practice of what one has learnt, and you said, ‘There may be a father or elder brother still alive’; but when Yen Yu asked the same question, you answered, ‘Yes, do so.’ I am at a loss to understand you, and venture to ask what you meant.”

The Master replied, “Yen Yu backs out of his duties; therefore I push him on. Tsz-lu has forwardness enough for them both; therefore I hold him back.”

On the occasion of that time of fear in K’wang, Yen Yuen having fallen behind, the Master said to him (afterwards), “I took it for granted you were a dead man.” “How should I dare to die,” said he, “while you, sir, still lived?"

On Ki Tsz-jen putting to him a question anent Tsz-lu and Yen Yu, as to whether they might be called "great ministers," the Master answered, "I had expected your question, sir, to be about something extraordinary, and lo! it is only about these two. Those whom we call 'great ministers' are such as serve their prince conscientiously, and who, when they cannot do so, retire. At present, as regards the two you ask about, they may be called 'qualified ministers.'"

"Well, are they then," he asked, "such as will follow their leader?"

"They would not follow him who should slay his father and his prince!" was the reply.

Through the intervention of Tsz-lu, Tsz-kau was being appointed governor of Pi.

"You are spoiling a good man's son," said the Master.

Tsz-lu rejoined, "But he will have the people and their superiors to gain experience from, and there will be the altars; what need to read books? He can become a student afterwards."

"Here is the reason for my hatred of glib-tongued people," said the Master.

On one occasion Tsz-lu, Tsang Sin, Yen Yu, and Kung-si Hwa were sitting near him. He said to them, "Though I may be a day older than you, do not (for the moment) regard me as such. While you are living this unoccupied life you are saying, 'We do not become known.' Now suppose some one got to know you, what then?"

Tsz-lu – first to speak – at once answered, "Give me a State of large size and armament, hemmed in and hampered by other larger States, the population augmented by armies and regiments, causing a dearth in it of food of all kinds; give me charge of that State, and in three years' time I should make a brave country of it, and let it know its place."

The Master smiled at him. "Yen," said he, "how would it be with you?"

"Give me," said Yen, "a territory of sixty or

seventy li square, or of fifty or sixty square; put me in charge of that, and in three years I should make the people sufficiently prosperous. As regards their knowledge of ceremonial or music, I should wait for superior men to teach them that."

"And with you, Kung-si, how would it be?"

This disciple's reply was, "I have nothing to say about my capabilities for such matters; my wish is to learn. I should like to be a junior assistant, in dark robe and cap, at the services of the ancestral temple, and at the Grand Receptions of the Princes by the Sovereign."

"And with you, Tsang Sin?"

This disciple was strumming on his harpsichord, but now the twanging ceased, he turned from the instrument, rose to his feet, and answered thus: "Something different from the choice of these three." "What harm?" said the Master; "I want each one of you to tell me what his heart is set upon." "Well, then," said he, "give me – in the latter part of spring – dressed in full spring-tide attire – in company with five or six young fellows of twenty,[27] or six or seven lads under that age, to do the ablutions in the stream, enjoy a breeze in the rain-dance,[28] and finish up with songs on the road home."

The Master drew in his breath, sighed, and exclaimed, "Ah, I take with you!"

The three other disciples having gone out, leaving Tsang Sin behind, the latter said, "What think you of the answers of those three?" – "Well, each told me what was uppermost in his mind," said the Master; – "simply that."

"Why did you smile at Tsz-lu, sir?"

"I smiled at him because to have the charge of a State requires due regard to the Rules of Propriety, and his words betrayed

---

27 Lit., capped ones. At twenty they underwent the ceremony of capping, and were considered men.

28 I.e., before the altars, where offerings were placed with prayer for rain. A religious dance.

a lack of modesty."

"But Yen, then – he had a State in view, had he not?"

"I should like to be shown a territory such as he described which does not amount to a State."

"But had not Kung-si also a State in view?"

"What are ancestral temples and Grand Receptions, but for the feudal lords to take part in? If Kung-si were to become an unimportant assistant at these functions, who could become an important one?"

BOOK TWELVE

The Master's Answers – Philanthropy – Friendships

YEN YUEN WAS ASKING about man's proper regard for his fellow-man. The Master said to him, "Self-control, and a habit of falling back upon propriety, virtually effect it. Let these conditions be fulfilled for one day, and every one round will betake himself to the duty. Is it to begin in one's self, or think you, indeed! it is to begin in others?"

"I wanted you to be good enough," said Yen Yuen, "to give me a brief synopsis of it."

Then said the Master, "Without Propriety use not your eyes; without it use not your ears, nor your tongue, nor a limb of your body."

"I may be lacking in diligence," said Yen Yuen, "but with your favor I will endeavor to carry out this advice."

Chung-kung asked about man's proper regard for his fellows.

To him the Master replied thus: "When you go forth from your door, be as if you were meeting some guest of importance. When you are making use of the common people (for State purposes), be as if you were taking part in a great religious function. Do not set before others what you do not desire yourself. Let there be no resentful feelings against you when you are away in the country, and none when at home."

"I may lack diligence," said Chung-kung,

"but with your favor I will endeavor to carry out this advice."

Sz-ma Niu asked the like question. The answer he received was this: "The words of the man who has a proper regard for his fellows are uttered with difficulty."

"'His words – uttered with difficulty?'" he echoed, in surprise. "Is that what is meant by proper regard for one's fellow-creatures?"

"Where there is difficulty in doing," the Master replied, "will there not be some difficulty in utterance?"

The same disciple put a question about the "superior man." "Superior men," he replied, "are free from trouble and apprehension."

"'Free from trouble and apprehension!'" said he. "Does that make them 'superior men'?"

The Master added, "Where there is found, upon introspection, to be no chronic disease, how shall there be any trouble? how shall there be any apprehension?"

The same disciple, being in trouble,

remarked, "I am alone in having no brother, while all else have theirs – younger or elder."

Tsz-hiŠ said to him, "I have heard this: 'Death and life have destined times; wealth and honors rest with Heaven. Let the superior man keep watch over himself without ceasing, showing deference to others, with propriety of manners – and all within the four seas will be his brethren. How should he be distressed for lack of brothers!'"[29]

Tsz-chang asked what sort of man might be termed "enlightened."

The Master replied, "That man with whom drenching slander and cutting calumny gain no currency may well be called enlightened. Ay, he with whom such things make no way may well be called enlightened in the extreme."

Tsz-kung put a question relative to

---

29 From Confucius, it is generally thought.

government. In reply the Master mentioned three essentials: – sufficient food, sufficient armament, and the people's confidence.

"But," said the disciple, "if you cannot really have all three, and one has to be given up, which would you give up first?"

"The armament," he replied.

"And if you are obliged to give up one of the remaining two, which would it be?"

"The food," said he. "Death has been the portion of all men from of old. Without the people's trust nothing can stand."

Kih Tsz-shing once said, "Give me the inborn qualities of a gentleman, and I want no more. How are such to come from book-learning?"

Tsz-kung exclaimed, "Ah! sir, I regret to hear such words from you. A gentleman! – But 'a team of four can ne'er o'er-take the tongue!' Literary accomplishments are much the same as inborn qualities, and inborn qualities as literary accomplishments. A tiger's or leopard's skin without the hair might be a dog's or sheep's when so made bare."

Duke Ngai was consulting Yu Joh. Said he, "It is a year of dearth, and there is an insufficiency for Ways and Means – what am I to do?"

"Why not apply the Tithing Statute?" said the minister.

"But two tithings would not be enough for my purposes," said the duke; "what would be the good of applying the Statute?"

The minister replied, "So long as the people have enough left for themselves, who of them will allow their prince to be without enough? But – when the people have not enough, who will allow their prince all that he wants?"

Tsz-chang was asking how the standard of virtue was to be raised, and how to discern what was illusory or misleading. The Master's answer was, "Give a foremost place to honesty and faithfulness, and tread the path of righteousness, and you will raise the standard of virtue. As to discerning what is illusory, here is an example of an illusion: – Whom you love you wish to live; whom you hate you wish to die. To have wished the same person to live and also to be dead – there is an illusion for you."

Duke King of Ts'i consulted Confucius about government. His answer was, "Let a prince be a prince, and ministers be ministers; let fathers be fathers, and sons be sons."

"Good!" exclaimed the duke; "truly if a prince fail to be a prince, and ministers to be ministers, and if fathers be not fathers, and sons not sons, then, even though I may have my allowance of grain, should I ever be able to relish it?"

"The man to decide a cause with half a word," exclaimed the Master, "is Tsz-lu!"

Tsz-lu never let a night pass between promise and performance.

"In hearing causes, I am like other men," said the Master. "The great point is – to prevent litigation."

Tsz-chang having raised some question about government, the Master said to him, "In the settlement of its principles be unwearied; in its administration – see to that loyally."

"The man of wide research," said he, "who also restrains himself by the Rules of Propriety, is not likely to transgress."

Again, "The noble-minded man makes the most of others' good qualities, not the worst of their bad ones. Men of small mind do the reverse of this."

Ki K'ang was consulting him about the direction of public affairs. Confucius answered him, "A director should be himself correct. If you, sir, as a leader show correctness, who will dare not to be correct?"

Ki K'ang, being much troubled on account of robbers abroad, consulted Confucius on the matter. He received this reply: "If you, sir, were not covetous, neither would they steal, even were you to bribe them to do so."

Ki K'ang, when consulting Confucius about the government, said, "Suppose I were to put to death the disorderly for the better encouragement of the orderly – what say you to that?"

"Sir," replied Confucius, "in the administration of government why resort to capital punishment? Covet what is good, and the people will be good. The virtue of the noble-minded man is as the wind, and that of inferior men as grass; the grass must bend, when the wind blows upon it."

Tsz-chang asked how otherwise he would describe the learned official who might be termed influential.

"What, I wonder, do you mean by one who is influential?" said the Master.

"I mean," replied the disciple, "one who is sure to have a reputation throughout the country, as well as at home."

"That," said the Master, "is reputation, not influence. The influential man, then, if he be one who is genuinely straightforward and loves what is just and right, a discriminator of men's words, and an observer of their looks, and in honor careful to prefer others to himself – will certainly have influence, both throughout the country and at home. The man of mere reputation, on the other hand, who speciously affects philanthropy, though in his way of procedure he acts contrary to it, while yet quite evidently engrossed with that virtue – will certainly have reputation, both in the country and at home."

Fan Ch'i, strolling with him over the ground below the place of the rain-dance, said to him, "I venture to ask how to raise the standard of virtue, how to reform dissolute habits, and how to discern what is illusory?"

"Ah! a good question indeed!" he exclaimed. "Well, is not putting duty first, and success second, a way of raising the standard of virtue? And is not attacking the evil in one's self, and not the evil which is in others, a way of reforming dissolute habits?

And as to illusions, is not one morning's fit of anger, causing a man to forget himself, and even involving in the consequences those who are near and dear to him – is not that an illusion?"

The same disciple asked him what was meant by "a right regard for one's fellow-creatures." He replied, "It is love to man."

Asked by him again what was meant by wisdom, he replied, "It is knowledge of man."

Fan Ch'i did not quite grasp his meaning.

The Master went on to say, "Lift up the straight, set aside the crooked, so can you make the crooked straight."

Fan Ch'i left him, and meeting with Tsz-hiŠ he said, "I had an interview just now with the Master, and I asked him what wisdom was. In his answer he said, 'Lift up the straight, set aside the crooked, and so can you make the crooked straight.' What was his meaning?"

"Ah! words rich in meaning, those," said the other. "When Shun was emperor, and was selecting his men from among the multitude, he ‘lifted up’ KŠu-yŠu; and men devoid of right feelings towards their kind went far away. And when T’ang was emperor, and chose out his men from the crowd, he ‘lifted up’ I-yin – with the same result.”

Tsz-kung was consulting him about a friend. “Speak to him frankly, and respectfully,” said the Master, “and gently lead him on. If you do not succeed, then stop; do not submit yourself to indignity.”

The learned Tsang observed, “In the society of books the ‘superior man’ collects his friends; in the society of his friends he is furthering good-will among men.”

BOOK THIRTEEN

Answers on the Art of Governing – Consistency

TSZ-LU WAS ASKING about government. "Lead the way in it," said the Master, "and work hard at it."

Requested to say more, he added, "And do not tire of it."

Chung-kung, on being made first minister to the Chief of the Ki family, consulted the

Master about government, and to him he said, "Let the heads of offices be heads. Excuse small faults. Promote men of sagacity and talent."

"But," he asked, "how am I to know the sagacious and talented, before promoting them?"

"Promote those whom you do know," said the Master.

"As to those of whom you are uncertain, will others omit to notice them?"

Tsz-lu said to the Master, "As the prince of Wei, sir, has been waiting for you to act for him in his government, what is it your intention to take in hand first?"

"One thing of necessity," he answered – "the rectification of terms."

"That!" exclaimed Tsz-lu. "How far away you are, sir! Why such rectification?"

"What a rustic you are, Tsz-lu!" rejoined the Master. "A gentleman would be a little reserved and reticent in matters which he does not understand. If terms be incorrect, language will be incongruous; and if language be incongruous, deeds will be imperfect. So, again, when deeds are imperfect, propriety and harmony cannot prevail, and when this is the case laws relating to crime will fail in their aim; and if these last so fail, the people will not know where to set hand or foot. Hence, a man of superior mind, certain first of his terms, is fitted to speak; and being certain of what he says can proceed upon it. In the language of such a person there is nothing heedlessly irregular – and that is the sum of the matter."

Fan Ch'i requested that he might learn something of husbandry. "For that." said the Master, "I am not equal to an old husbandman." Might he then learn something of gardening? he asked. "I am not equal to an old gardener." was the reply.

"A man of little mind, that!" said the Master, when Fan Ch'i had gone out. "Let a man who is set over the people love propriety, and they will not presume to be disrespectful. Let him be a lover of righteousness, and they will not presume to be aught but submissive. Let him love faithfulness and truth, and they will not presume not to lend him their hearty assistance. Ah, if all this only were so, the people from all sides would come to such a one, carrying their children on their backs. What need to turn his hand to husbandry?

"Though a man," said he, "could hum through the Odes – the three hundred – yet should show himself unskilled when given some administrative work to do for his country; though he might know much of that other lore, yet if, when sent on a mission to any quarter, he could answer no question personally and unaided, what after all is he good for?

"Let a leader," said he, "show rectitude in his own personal character, and even without directions from him things will go well. If he be not personally upright, his directions will not be complied with."

Once he made the remark, "The

governments of Lu and of Wei are in brotherhood."

Of King, a son of the Duke of Wei, he observed that "he managed his household matters well. On his coming into possession, he thought, 'What a strange conglomeration!' – Coming to possess a little more, it was, 'Strange, such a result!' And when he became wealthy, 'Strange, such elegance!'"

The Master was on a journey to Wei, and Yen Yu was driving him. "What multitudes of people!" he exclaimed. Yen Yu asked him, "Seeing they are so numerous, what more would you do for them?"

"Enrich them," replied the Master.

"And after enriching them, what more would you do for them?"

"Instruct them."

"Were any one of our princes to employ me," he said, "after a twelvemonth I might have made some tolerable progress;"

Again, "How true is that saying, 'Let good

men have the management of a country for a century, and they would be adequate to cope with evil-doers, and thus do away with capital punishments,'"

Again, "Suppose the ruler to possess true kingly qualities, then surely after one generation there would be good-will among men."

Again, "Let a ruler but see to his own rectitude, and what trouble will he then have in the work before him? If he be unable to rectify himself, how is he to rectify others?"

Once when Yen Yu was leaving the Court, the Master accosted him. "Why so late?" he asked. "Busy with legislation," Yen replied. "The details of it," suggested the Master; "had it been legislation, I should have been there to hear it, even though I am not in office."

Duke Ting asked if there were one sentence which, if acted upon, might have the effect of making a country prosperous.

Confucius answered, "A sentence could

hardly be supposed to do so much as that. But there is a proverb people use which says, 'To play the prince is hard, to play the minister not easy.' Assuming that it is understood that 'to play the prince is hard,' would it not be probable that with that one sentence the country should be made to prosper?"

"Is there, then," he asked, "one sentence which, if acted upon, would have the effect of ruining a country?"

Confucius again replied, "A sentence could hardly be supposed to do so much as that. But there is a proverb men have which says, 'Not gladly would I play the prince, unless my words were ne'er withstood.' Assuming that the words were good, and that none withstood them, would not that also be good? But assuming that they were not good, and yet none withstood them, would it not be probable that with that one saying he would work his country's ruin?"

When the Duke of Sheh consulted him about government, he replied, "Where the near are gratified, the far will follow."

When Tsz-hiŠ became governor of KŁ-fu, and consulted him about government, he answered, "Do not wish for speedy results. Do not look at trivial advantages. If you wish for speedy results, they will not be far-reaching; and if you regard trivial advantages you will not successfully deal with important affairs."

The Duke of Sheh in a conversation with Confucius said, "There are some straightforward persons in my neighborhood. If a father has stolen a sheep, the son will give evidence against him."

"Straightforward people in my neighborhood are different from those," said Confucius. "The father will hold a thing secret on his son's behalf, and the son does the same for his father. They are on their way to becoming straightforward."

Fan Ch'i was asking him about duty to one's fellow-men. "Be courteous," he replied, "in your private sphere; be serious in any duty you take in hand to do; be leal-hearted in your intercourse with others. Even though you were to go amongst the wild tribes, it would not be right for you to neglect these duties."

In answer to Tsz-kung, who asked, "how he would characterize one who could fitly be called 'learned official,'" the Master said, "He may be so-called who in his private life is affected with a sense of his own unworthiness, and who, when sent on a mission to any quarter of the empire, would not disgrace his prince's commands."

"May I presume," said his questioner, "to ask what sort you would put next to such?"

"Him who is spoken of by his kinsmen as a dutiful son, and whom the folks of his neighborhood call' good brother.'"

"May I still venture to ask whom you would place next in order?"

"Such as are sure to be true to their word, and effective in their work – who are given to hammering, as it were, upon one note –

of inferior calibre indeed, but fit enough, I think, to be ranked next."

"How would you describe those who are at present in the government service?"

"Ugh! mere peck and panier men! – not worth taking into the reckoning."

Once he remarked, "If I cannot get **via media** men to impart instruction to, then I must of course take the impetuous and undisciplined! The impetuous ones will at least go forward and lay hold on things; and the undisciplined have at least something in them which needs to be brought out."

"The Southerners," said he, "have the proverb, 'The man who sticks not to rule will never make a charm-worker or a medical man,' Good! – 'Whoever is intermittent in his practise of virtue will live to be ashamed of it.' Without prognostication," he added, "that will indeed be so."

"The nobler-minded man," he remarked, "will be agreeable even when he disagrees; the small-minded man will agree and be disagreeable."

Tsz-kung was consulting him, and asked, "What say you of a person who was liked by all in his village?"

"That will scarcely do," he answered.

"What, then, if they all disliked him?"

"That, too," said he, "is scarcely enough. Better if he were liked by the good folk in the village, and disliked by the bad."

"The superior man," he once observed, "is easy to serve, but difficult to please. Try to please him by the adoption of wrong principles, and you will fail. Also, when such a one employs others, he uses them according to their capacity. The inferior man is, on the other hand, difficult to serve, but easy to please. Try to please him by the adoption of wrong principles, and you will succeed. And when he employs others he requires them to be fully prepared for everything."

Again, "The superior man can be high without being haughty. The inferior man can be haughty if not high."

"The firm, the unflinching, the plain and simple, the slow to speak," said he once, "are approximating towards their duty to their fellow-men."

Tsz-lu asked how he would characterize one who might fitly be called an educated gentleman. The master replied, "He who can properly be so-called will have in him a seriousness of purpose, a habit of controlling himself, and an agreeableness of manner: among his friends and associates the seriousness and the self-control, and among his brethren the agreeableness of manner."

"Let good and able men discipline the people for seven years," said the Master, "and after that they may do to go to war."

But, said he, "To lead an undisciplined people to war – that I call throwing them away."

BOOK FOURTEEN

Good and Bad Government – Miscellaneous Sayings

YUEN SZ ASKED WHAT might be considered to bring shame on one.

"Pay," said the Master; "pay – ever looking to that, whether the country be well or badly governed."

"When imperiousness, boastfulness, resentments, and covetousness cease to prevail among the people, may it be considered that mutual good-will has been effected?" To this question the Master replied, "A hard thing overcome, it may be considered. But as to the mutual good-will – I cannot tell."

"Learned officials," said he, "who hanker after a home life, are not worthy of being esteemed as such."

Again, "In a country under good government, speak boldly, act boldly. When the land is ill-governed, though you act boldly, let your words be moderate."

Again, "Men of virtue will needs be men of words – will speak out – but men of words are not necessarily men of virtue. They who care for their fellow-men will needs be bold, but the bold may not necessarily be such as care for their fellow-men."

Nan-kung Kwoh, who was consulting Confucius, observed respecting I, the skilful archer, and Ngau, who could propel a boat on dry land, that neither of them died a natural death; while Yu and Tsih, who with their own hands had labored at husbandry, came to wield imperial sway.

The Master gave him no reply. But when the speaker had gone out he exclaimed, "A superior man, that! A man who values virtue, that!"

"There have been noble-minded men," said he, "who yet were wanting in philanthropy; but never has there been a small-minded man who had philanthropy in him."

He asked, "Can any one refuse to toil for those he loves? Can any one refuse to exhort, who is true-hearted?"

Speaking of the preparation of Government Notifications in his day he said, "P'i would draw up a rough sketch of what was to be said; the Shishuh then looked it carefully through and put it into proper shape; Tsz-yu next, who was master of the ceremonial of State intercourse, improved and adorned its phrases; and Tsz-ch'an of Tung-li added his scholarly embellishments thereto."

To some one who asked his opinion of the last-named, he said, "He was a kind-hearted man." Asked what he thought of Tsz-si, he exclaimed, "Alas for him! alas for him!" – Asked again about Kwan Chung, his answer was, "As to him, he once seized the town of P'in with its three hundred families from the Chief of the Pih clan, who, afterwards reduced to living upon coarse rice, with all his teeth gone, never uttered a word of complaint."

"It is no light thing," said he, "to endure poverty uncomplainingly; and a difficult thing to bear wealth without becoming arrogant."

Respecting Mang Kung-ch'oh, he said that, while he was fitted for something better than the post of chief officer in the ChŠu or Wei families, he was not competent to act as minister in small States like those of T'ang or Sieh.

Tsz-lu asked how he would describe a perfect man. He replied, "Let a man have the sagacity of Tsang Wu-chung, the freedom from covetousness of Kung-ch'oh, the boldness of Chwang of P'in, and the attainments in polite arts of Yen Yu; and gift him further with the graces taught by the 'Books of Rites' and 'Music' – then he may be considered a perfect man. But," said he, "what need of such in these days? The man that may be regarded as perfect now is the one who, seeing some advantage to himself, is mindful of righteousness; who, seeing danger, risks his life; and who, if bound by some covenant of long standing, never forgets its conditions as life goes on."

Respecting Kung-shuh Wan, the Master inquired of Kung-ming KiŠ, saying, "Is it true that your master never speaks, never laughs, never takes aught from others?"

"Those who told you that of him," said he, "have gone too far. My master speaks when there is occasion to do so, and men are not surfeited with his speaking. When there is occasion to be merry too, he will laugh, but men have never overmuch of his laughing. And whenever it is just and right to take things from others, he will take them, but never so as to allow men to think him burdensome." "Is that the case with him?" said the Master. "Can it be so?"

Respecting Tsang Wu-chung the Master said, "When he sought from Lu the appointment of a successor to him, and for this object held on to his possession of the fortified city of Fang – if you say he was not then using constraint towards his prince, I must refuse to believe it."

Duke Wan of Tsin he characterized as "artful but not upright"; and Duke Hwan of Ts'i as "upright but not artful."

Tsz-lu remarked, "When Duke Hwan caused his brother Kiu to be put to death, Shau Hwuh committed suicide, but Kwan Chung did not. I should say he was not a man who had much good-will in him – eh?"

The Master replied, "When Duke Hwan held a great gathering of the feudal lords, dispensing with military equipage, it was owing to Kwan Chung's energy that such an event was brought about. Match such good-will as that – match it if you can."

Tsz-kung then spoke up. "But was not Kwan Chung wanting in good-will? He could not give up his life when Duke Hwan caused his brother to be put to death. Besides, he became the duke's counsellor."

"And in acting as his counsellor put him at the head of all the feudal lords," said the Master, "and unified and reformed the whole empire; and the people, even to this day, reap benefit from what he did. Had it not been for him we should have been going about with locks unkempt and buttoning our jackets (like barbarians) on the left. Would you suppose that he should show the same sort of attachment as exists between a poor yokel and his one wife – that he would asphyxiate himself in some sewer, leaving no one the wiser?"

Kung-shuh Wan's steward, who became the high officer Sien, went up accompanied by Wan to the prince's hall of audience.

When Confucius heard of this he remarked, "He may well be esteemed a 'Wan.'"

The Master having made some reference to the lawless ways of Duke Ling of Wei, Ki K'ang said to him, "If he be like that, how is it he does not ruin his position?"

Confucius answered, "The Chung-shuh, Yu, is charged with the entertainment of visitors and strangers; the priest T'o has charge of the ancestral temple; and Wang-sun KiŠ has the control of the army and its divisions: – with men such as those, how should he come to ruin?"

He once remarked, "He who is unblushing in his words will with difficulty substantiate them."

Ch'in Shing had slain Duke Kien. Hearing of this, Confucius, after performing his ablutions, went to Court and announced the news to Duke Ngai, saying, "Ch'in Hang has slain his prince. May I request that you proceed against him?"

"Inform the Chiefs of the Three Families," said the duke.

Soliloquizing upon this, Confucius said, "Since he uses me to back his ministers,[30] I did not dare not to announce the matter to him; and now he says, 'Inform the Three Chiefs.'"

He went to the Three Chiefs and informed them, but nothing could be done. Whereupon again he said, "Since he uses me to back his ministers, I did not dare not to announce the matter."

Tsz-lu was questioning him as to how he should serve his prince. "Deceive him not, but reprove him," he answered.

"The minds of superior men," he observed, "trend upwards; those of inferior men trend downwards."

Again, "Students of old fixed their eyes

---

30 Confucius had now retired from office, and this incident occurred only two years before his death.

upon themselves: now they learn with their eyes upon others."

KŁ Pih-yuh despatched a man with a message to Confucius. Confucius gave him a seat, and among other inquiries he asked, "How is your master managing?" "My master," he replied, "has a great wish to be seldom at fault, and as yet he cannot manage it."

"What a messenger!" exclaimed he admiringly, when the man went out. "What a messenger!"

"When not occupying the office," was a remark of his, "devise not the policy."

The Learned Tsang used to say, "The thoughts of the 'superior man' do not wander from his own office."

"Superior men," said the Master, "are modest in their words, profuse in their deeds."

Again, "There are three attainments of the superior man which are beyond me – the being sympathetic without anxiety, wise without scepticism, brave without fear."

"Sir," said Tsz-kung, "that is what you say of yourself."

Whenever Tsz-kung drew comparisons from others, the Master would say, "Ah, how wise and great you must have become! Now I have no time to do that."

Again, "My great concern is, not that men do not know me, but that they cannot."

Again, "If a man refrain from making preparations against his being imposed upon, and from counting upon others' want of good faith towards him, while he is foremost to perceive what is passing – surely that is a wise and good man."

Wi-shang Mau accosted Confucius, saying, "Kiu, how comes it that you manage to go perching and roosting in this way? Is it not because you show yourself so smart a speaker, now?"

"I should not dare do that," said Confucius. "Tis that I am sick of men's immovableness and deafness to reason."

"In a well-bred horse," said he, "what one admires is not its speed, but its good points."

Some one asked, "What say you of the remark, 'Requite enmity with kindness'?"

"How then," he answered, "would you requite kindness? Requite enmity with straightforwardness, and kindness with kindness."

"Ah! no one knows me!" he once exclaimed.

"Sir," said Tsz-kung, "how comes it to pass that no one knows you?"

"While I murmur not against Heaven," continued the Master, "nor cavil at men; while I stoop to learn and aspire to penetrate into things that are high; yet 'tis Heaven alone knows what I am."

LiŠu, a kinsman of the duke, having laid a complaint against Tsz-lu before Ki K'ang, an officer came to Confucius to inform him of the fact, and he added, "My lord is certainly having his mind poisoned by his kinsman LiŠu, but through my influence perhaps we may yet manage to see him exposed in the marketplace or the Court."

"If right principles are to have their course, it is so destined," said the Master; "if they are not to have their course, it is so destined. What can LiŠu do against Destiny?"

"There are worthy men," said the Master, "fleeing from the world; some from their district; some from the sight of men's looks; some from the language they hear."

"The men who have risen from their posts and withdrawn in this manner are seven in number."

Tsz-lu, having lodged overnight in Shih-mun, was accosted by the gate-keeper in the morning. "Where from?" he asked. "From Confucius," Tsz-lu responded. "That is the man," said he, "who knows things are not up to the mark, and is making some ado about them, is it not?"

When the Master was in Wei, he was once pounding on the musical stone, when a man with a basket of straw crossed his threshold, and exclaimed, "Ah, there is a heart that feels! Aye, drub the stone!" After which he added, "How vulgar! how he hammers away on one note! – and no one knows him, and he gives up, and all is over!

Be it deep, our skirts we'll raise to the waist,
– Or shallow, then up to the knee,'"

"What determination!" said the Master. "Yet it was not hard to do."

Tsz-chang once said to him, "In the 'Book of the Annals' it is stated that while KŠu-tsung was in the Mourning Shed he spent the three years without speaking. What is meant by that?"

"Why must you name KŠu-tsung?" said the Master. "It was so with all other ancient sovereigns: when one of them died, the heads of every department agreed between themselves that they should give ear for three years to the Prime Minister."

"When their betters love the Rules, then

the folk are easy tools," was a saying of the Master.

Tsz-lu having asked what made a "superior man," he answered, "Self-culture, with a view to becoming seriously-minded."

"Nothing more than that?" said he.

"Self-culture with a view to the greater satisfaction of others," added the Master.

"That, and yet no more?"

"Self-culture with a view to the greater satisfaction of all the clans and classes," he again added. "Self-culture for the sake of all – a result that, that would almost put Yau and Shun into the shade!"

To Yuen Jang,[31] who was sitting waiting for him in a squatting (disrespectful) posture, the Master delivered himself as follows: "The man who in his youth could show no

---

[31] It is a habit with the Chinese, when a number are out walking together, for the eldest to go first, the others pairing off according to their age. It is a custom much older than the time of Confucius.

humility or subordination, who in his prime misses his opportunity, and who when old age comes upon him will not die – that man is a miscreant." And he tapped him on the shin with his staff.

Some one asked about his attendant – a youth from the village of Kiueh – whether he was one who improved. He replied, "I note that he seats himself in the places reserved for his betters, and that when he is walking he keeps abreast with his seniors. He is not one of those who care for improvement: he wants to be a man all at once."

BOOK FIFTEEN

Practical Wisdom – Reciprocity the Rule of Life

DUKE LING OF WEI was consulting Confucius about army arrangements. His answer was, “Had you asked me about such things as temple requisites, I have learnt that business, but I have not yet studied military matters.” And he followed up this reply by leaving on the following day.

After this, during his residence in the State of Ch'in, his followers, owing to a stoppage of food supply, became so weak and ill that not one of them could stand. Tsz-lu, with indignation pictured on his countenance, exclaimed, "And is a gentleman to suffer starvation?"

"A gentleman," replied the Master, "will endure it unmoved, but a common person breaks out into excesses under it."

Addressing Tsz-kung, the Master said, "You regard me as one who studies and stores up in his mind a multiplicity of things – do you not?" – "I do," he replied; "is it not so?" – "Not at all. I have one idea – one cord on which to string all."

To Tsz-lu he remarked, "They who know Virtue are rare."

"If you would know one who without effort ruled well, was not Shun such a one? What did he indeed do? He bore himself with reverent dignity and undeviatingly 'faced the south,' and that was all."

Tsz-chang was consulting him about making way in life. He answered, "Be true and honest in all you say, and seriously earnest in all you do, and then, even if your country be one inhabited by barbarians, South or North, you will make your way. If you do not show yourself thus in word and deed how should you succeed, even in your own district or neighborhood? – When you are afoot, let these two counsels be two companions preceding you, yourself viewing them from behind; when you drive, have them in view as on the yoke of your carriage. Then may you make your way."

Tsz-chang wrote them on the two ends of his cincture.

"Straight was the course of the Annalist Yu," said the Master – "aye, straight as an arrow flies; were the country well governed or ill governed, his was an arrow-like course.

"A man of masterly mind, too, is KŁ Pih-yuh! When the land is being rightly governed he will serve; when it is under bad government he is apt to recoil, and brood."

"Not to speak to a man." said he, "to whom you ought to speak, is to lose your man; to speak to one to whom you ought not to speak is to lose your words. Those who are wise will not lose their man nor yet their words."

Again, "The scholar whose heart is in his work, and who is philanthropic, seeks not to gain a livelihood by any means that will do harm to his philanthropy. There have been men who have destroyed their own lives in the endeavor to bring that virtue in them to perfection."

Tsz-kung asked how to become philanthropic. The Master answered him thus: "A workman who wants to do his work well must first sharpen his tools. In whatever land you live, serve under some wise and good man among those in high office, and make friends with the more humane of its men of education."

Yen Yuen consulted him on the

management of a country. He answered: –

"Go by the HiŠ Calendar. Have the State carriages like those of the Yin princes. Wear the Chow cap. For your music let that of Shun be used for the posturers. Put away the songs of Ch'ing, and remove far from you men of artful speech: the Ch'ing songs are immodest, and artful talkers are dangerous."

Other sayings of the Master: –

"They who care not for the morrow will the sooner have their sorrow.

"Ah, 'tis hopeless! I have not yet met with the man who loves Virtue as he loves Beauty.

"Was not Tsang Wan like one who surreptitiously came by the post he held? He knew the worth of Hwḳi of Liu-hiŠ, and could not stand in his presence.

"Be generous yourself, and exact little from others; then you banish complaints.

"With one who does not come to me inquiring 'What of this?' and 'What of that?'

I never can ask 'What of this?' and give him up.

"If a number of students are all day together, and in their conversation never approach the subject of righteousness, but are fond merely of giving currency to smart little sayings, they are difficult indeed to manage.

"When the 'superior man' regards righteousness as the thing material, gives operation to it according to the Rules of Propriety, lets it issue in humility, and become complete in sincerity – there indeed is your superior man!

"The trouble of the superior man will be his own want of ability: it will be no trouble to him that others do not know him.

"Such a man thinks it hard to end his days and leave a name to be no longer named.

"The superior man is exacting of himself; the common man is exacting of others.

"A superior man has self-respect, and does not strive; is sociable, yet no party man.

"He does not promote a man because of

his words, or pass over the words because of the man."

Tsz-kung put to him the question, "Is there one word upon which the whole life may proceed?"

The Master replied, "Is not Reciprocity such a word? – what you do not yourself desire, do not put before others."

"So far as I have to do with others, whom do I over-censure? whom do I over-praise? If there be something in them that looks very praiseworthy, that something I put to the test. I would have the men of the present day to walk in the straight path whereby those of the Three Dynasties have walked.

"I have arrived as it were at the annalist's blank page. – Once he who had a horse would lend it to another to mount; now, alas! it is not so.

"Artful speech is the confusion of Virtue. Impatience over little things introduces confusion into great schemes.

"What is disliked by the masses needs

inquiring into; so also does that which they have a preference for.

"A man may give breadth to his principles: it is not principles (in themselves) that give breadth to the man.

"Not to retract after committing an error may itself be called error.

"If I have passed the whole day without food and the whole night without sleep, occupied with my thoughts, it profits me nothing: I were better engaged in learning.

"The superior man deliberates upon how he may walk in truth, not upon what he may eat. The farmer may plough, and be on the way to want: the student learns, and is on his way to emolument. To live a right life is the concern of men of nobler minds: poverty gives them none.

"Whatsoever the intellect may attain to, unless the humanity within is powerful enough to keep guard over it, is assuredly lost, even though it be gained.

"If there be intellectual attainments, and the

humanity within is powerful enough to keep guard over them, yet, unless (in a ruler) there be dignity in his rule, the people will fail to show him respect.

"Again, given the intellectual attainments, and humanity sufficient to keep watch over them, and also dignity in ruling, yet if his movements be not in accordance with the Rules of Propriety, he is not yet fully qualified.

"The superior man may not be conversant with petty details, and yet may have important matters put into his hands. The inferior man may not be charged with important matters, yet may be conversant with the petty details.

"Good-fellowship is more to men than fire and water. I have seen men stepping into fire and into water, and meeting with death thereby; I have not yet seen a man die from planting his steps in the path of good-fellowship.

"Rely upon good nature. 'Twill not allow precedence even to a teacher.

"The superior man is inflexibly upright,

and takes not things upon trust.

"In serving your prince, make your service the serious concern, and let salary be a secondary matter.

"Where instruction is to be given, there must be no distinction of persons.

"Where men's methods are not identical, there can be no planning by one on behalf of another.

"In speaking, perspicuity is all that is needed."

When the blind music-master Mien paid him a visit, on his approaching the steps the Master called out "Steps," and on his coming to the mat, said "Mat." When all in the room were seated, the Master told him "So-and-so is here, so-and-so is here."

When the music-master had left, Tsz-chang said to him, "Is that the way to speak to the music-master?" "Well," he replied, "it is certainly the way to assist him."

BOOK SIXTEEN

Against Intestine Strife – Good and Bad Friendships

THE CHIEF OF THE Ki family was about to make an onslaught upon the Chuen-yu domain.

Yen Yu and Tsz-lu in an interview with Confucius told him, "The Ki is about to have an affair with Chuen-yu."

"Yen," said Confucius, "does not the fault

lie with you? The Chief of Chuen-yu in times past was appointed lord of the East Mung (mountain); besides, he dwells within the confines of your own State, and is an official of the State-worship; how can you think of making an onslaught upon him?"

"It is the wish of our Chief," said Yen Yu, "not the wish of either of us ministers."

Confucius said, "Yen, there is a sentence of ChŠu Jin which runs thus: 'Having made manifest their powers and taken their place in the official list, when they find themselves incompetent they resign; if they cannot be firm when danger threatens the government, nor lend support when it is reeling, of what use then shall they be as Assistants?' – Besides, you are wrong in what you said. When a rhinoceros or tiger breaks out of its cage – when a jewel or tortoise-shell ornament is damaged in its casket – whose fault is it?"

"But," said Yen Yu, "so far as Chuen-yu is concerned, it is now fortified, and it is close to

Pi; and if he does not now take it, in another generation it will certainly be a trouble to his descendants."

"Yen!" exclaimed Confucius, "it is a painful thing to a superior man to have to desist from saying, 'My wish is so-and-so,' and to be obliged to make apologies. For my part, I have learnt this – that rulers of States and heads of Houses are not greatly concerned about their small following, but about the want of equilibrium in it – that they do not concern themselves about their becoming poor, but about the best means of living quietly and contentedly; for where equilibrium is preserved there will be no poverty, where there is harmony their following will not be small, and where there is quiet contentment there will be no decline nor fall. Now if that be the case, it follows that if men in outlying districts are not submissive, then a reform in education and morals will bring them to; and when they have been so won, then will you render them quiet and contented. At the present time you two are Assistants of your Chief; the people in the outlying districts are not submissive, and cannot be brought round. Your dominion is divided, prostrate, dispersed, cleft in pieces, and you as its guardians are powerless. And plans are being made for taking up arms against those who dwell within your own State. I am apprehensive that the sorrow of the Ki family is not to lie in Chuen-yu, but in those within their own screen."

"When the empire is well-ordered," said Confucius, "it is from the emperor that edicts regarding ceremonial, music, and expeditions to quell rebellion go forth. When it is being ill governed, such edicts emanate from the feudal lords; and when the latter is the case, it will be strange if in ten generations there is not a collapse. If they emanate merely from the high officials, it will be strange if the collapse do not come in five generations. When the State-edicts are in the hands of the subsidiary ministers, it will be strange if in three generations there is no collapse.

"When the empire is well-ordered, government is not left in the hands of high officials.

"When the empire is well-ordered, the common people will cease to discuss public matters."

"For five generations," he said, "the revenue has departed from the ducal household. Four generations ago the government fell into the hands of the high officials. Hence, alas! the straitened means of the descendants of the three Hwan families."

"There are," said he, "three kinds of friendships which are profitable, and three which are detrimental. To make friends with the upright, with the trustworthy, with the experienced, is to gain benefit; to make friends with the subtly perverse, with the artfully pliant, with the subtle in speech, is detrimental."

Again, "There are three kinds of pleasure which are profitable, and three which are detrimental. To take pleasure in going regularly through the various branches of Ceremonial and Music, in speaking of others' goodness, in having many worthy wise friends, is profitable. To take pleasure in wild bold pleasures, in idling carelessly about, in the too jovial accompaniments of feasting, is detrimental."

Again, "Three errors there be, into which they who wait upon their superior may fall: – (1) to speak before the opportunity comes to them to speak, which I call heedless haste; (2) refraining from speaking when the opportunity has come, which I call concealment; and (3) speaking, regardless of the mood he is in, which I call blindness."

Again, "Three things a superior should guard against: – (1) against the lusts of the flesh in his earlier years while the vital powers are not fully developed and fixed; (2) against the spirit of combativeness when he has come to the age of robust manhood and when the vital powers are matured and strong, and (3) against ambitiousness when old age has come on and the vital powers have become weak and decayed."

"Three things also such a man greatly reveres: – (1) the ordinances of Heaven, (2) great men, (3) words of sages. The inferior man knows not the ordinances of Heaven and therefore reveres them not, is unduly familiar in the presence of great men, and scoffs at the words of sages."

"They whose knowledge comes by birth are of all men the first in understanding; they to whom it comes by study are next; men of poor intellectual capacity, who yet study, may be added as a yet inferior class; and lowest of all are they who are poor in intellect and never learn."

"Nine things there are of which the superior man should be mindful: – to be clear in vision, quick in hearing, genial in expression, respectful in demeanor, true in word, serious in duty, inquiring in doubt, firmly self-controlled in anger, just and fair when the way to success opens out before him."

"Some have spoken of 'looking upon goodness as upon something beyond their reach,' and of 'looking upon evil as like plunging one's hands into scalding liquid'; – I have seen the men, I have heard the sayings.

"Some, again, have talked of 'living in seclusion to work out their designs,' and of 'exercising themselves in righteous living in order to render their principles the more effective'; – I have heard the sayings, I have not seen the men."

"Duke King of Ts'i had his thousand teams of four, yet on the day of his death the people had nothing to say of his goodness. Peh-I and Shuh-Ts'i starved at the foot of Shau-yang, and the people make mention of them to this day.

'E'en if not wealth thine object be,
'Tis all the same, thou'rt changed to

me.'

"Is not this apropos in such cases?"

Tsz-k'in asked of Pih-yu, "Have you heard anything else peculiar from your father?"

"Not yet," said he. "Once, though, he was standing alone when I was hurrying past him over the vestibule, and he said, 'Are you studying the Odes?' 'Not yet,' I replied. 'If you do not learn the Odes,' said he, 'you will not have the wherewithal for conversing,' I turned away and studied the Odes. Another day, when he was again standing alone and I was hurrying past across the vestibule, he said to me, 'Are you learning the Rules of Propriety?' 'Not yet,' I replied. 'If you have not studied the Rules, you have nothing to stand upon,' said he. I turned away and studied the Rules. – These two things I have heard from him."

Tsz-k'in turned away, and in great glee exclaimed, "I asked one thing, and have got three. I have learnt something about the Odes, and about the Rules, and moreover

I have learnt how the superior man will turn away his own son."

The wife of the ruler of a State is called by her husband "My helpmeet." She speaks of herself as "Your little handmaiden." The people of that State call her "The prince's helpmeet," but addressing persons of another State they speak of her as "Our little princess." When persons of another State name her they say also "Your prince's helpmeet."

BOOK SEVENTEEN

The Master Induced to Take Office – Nature and Habit

YANG HO WAS DESIROUS of having an interview with Confucius, but on the latter's failing to go and see him, he sent a present of a pig to his house. Confucius went to return his acknowledgments for it at a time when he was not at home. They met, however, on the way.

He said to Confucius, "Come, I want a word with you. Can that man be said to have good-will towards his fellow-men who hugs and hides his own precious gifts and allows his country to go on in blind error?"

"He cannot," was the reply.

"And can he be said to be wise who, with a liking for taking part in the public service, is constantly letting slip his opportunities?"

"He cannot," was the reply again.

"And the days and months are passing; and the years do not wait for us."

"True," said Confucius; "I will take office."

It was a remark of the Master that while "by nature we approximate towards each other, by experience we go far asunder."

Again, "Only the supremely wise and the most deeply ignorant do not alter."

The Master once, on his arrival at Wu-shing, heard the sound of stringed instruments and singing. His face beamed with pleasure, and he said laughingly, "To kill a cock – why use an ox-knife?"

Tsz-yu, the governor, replied, “In former days, sir, I heard you say, ‘Let the superior man learn right principles, and he will be loving to other men; let the ordinary person learn right principles, and he will be easily managed.’”

The Master (turning to his disciples) said, “Sirs, what he says is right: what I said just now was only in play.”

Having received an invitation from Kung-shan Fuh-jau, who was in revolt against the government and was holding to his district of Pi, the Master showed an inclination to go.

Tsz-lu was averse to this, and said, “You can never go, that is certain; how should you feel you must go to that person?”

“Well,” said the Master, “he who has invited me must surely not have done so without a sufficient reason! And if it should happen that my services were enlisted, I might create for him another East Chow – don’t you think so?”

Tsz-chang asked Confucius about the virtue of philanthropy. His answer was, “It is the being able to put in practice five qualities, in any place under the sun.”

“May I ask, please, what these are?” said the disciple.

“They are,” he said, “dignity, indulgence, faithfulness, earnestness, kindness. If you show dignity you will not be mocked; if you are indulgent you will win the multitude; if faithful, men will place their trust in you; if earnest, you will do something meritorious; and if kind, you will be enabled to avail yourself amply of men’s services.”

Pih Hih sent the Master an invitation, and he showed an inclination to go.

Tsz-lu (seeing this) said to him, “In former days, sir, I have heard you say, ‘A superior man will not enter the society of one who does not that which is good in matters concerning himself’; and this man is in revolt, with Chung-man in his possession; if you go to him, how will the case stand?”

"Yes," said the Master, "those are indeed my words; but is it not said, 'What is hard may be rubbed without being made thin,' and 'White may be stained without being made black'? – I am surely not a gourd! How am I to be strung up like that kind of thing – and live without means?"

"Tsz-lu," said the Master, "you have heard of the six words with their six obfuscations?"

"No," said he, "not so far."

"Sit down, and I will tell you them. They are these six virtues, cared for without care for any study about them: – philanthropy, wisdom, faithfulness, straightforwardness, courage, firmness. And the six obfuscations resulting from not liking to learn about them are, respectively, these: – fatuity, mental dissipation, mischievousness, perversity, insubordination, impetuosity."

"My children," said he once, "why does no one of you study the Odes? – They are adapted to rouse the mind, to assist observation, to make people sociable, to arouse virtuous indignation. They speak of duties near and far – the duty of ministering to a parent, the duty of serving one's prince; and it is from them that one becomes conversant with the names of many birds, and beasts, and plants, and trees."

To his son Pih-yu he said, "Study you the Odes of Chow and the South, and those of Shau and the South. The man who studies not these is, I should say, somewhat in the position of one who stands facing a wall!"

"'Etiquette demands it.' 'Etiquette demands it,' so people plead," said he; "but do not these hankerings after jewels and silks indeed demand it? Or it is, 'The study of Music requires it' – 'Music requires it'; but do not these predilections for bells and drums require it?"

Again, "They who assume an outward appearance of severity, being inwardly weak, may be likened to low common men; nay, are they not somewhat like thieves that break through walls and steal?"

Again, "The plebeian kind of respect for piety is the very pest of virtue."

Again, "Listening on the road, and repeating in the lane – this is abandonment of virtue."

"Ah, the low-minded creatures!" he exclaimed. "How is it possible indeed to serve one's prince in their company? Before they have got what they wanted they are all anxiety to get it, and after they have got it they are all anxiety lest they should lose it; and while they are thus full of concern lest they should lose it, there is no length to which they will not go."

Again, "In olden times people had three moral infirmities; which, it may be, are now unknown. Ambitiousness in those olden days showed itself in momentary outburst; the ambitiousness of to-day runs riot. Austerity in those days had its sharp angles; in these it is irritable and perverse. Feebleness of intellect then was at least straightforward; in our day it is never aught but deceitful."

Again, "Rarely do we find mutual good

feeling where there is fine speech and studied mien."

Again, "To me it is abhorrent that purple color should be made to detract from that of vermilion. Also that the Odes of Ch'ing should be allowed to introduce discord in connection with the music of the Festal Songs and Hymns. Also that sharp-whetted tongues should be permitted to subvert governments."

Once said he, "Would that I could dispense with speech!"

"Sir," said Tsz-kung, "if you were never to speak, what should your pupils have to hand down from you?"

"Does Heaven ever speak?" said the Master. "The four seasons come and go, and all creatures live and grow. Does Heaven indeed speak?"

Once Ju Pi desired an interview with Confucius, from which the latter excused himself on the score of ill-health; but while the attendant was passing out through the doorway with the message he took his lute and sang, in such a way as to let him hear him.

Tsai Wo questioned him respecting the three years' mourning, saying that one full twelve-month was a long time – that, if gentlemen were for three years to cease from observing rules of propriety, propriety must certainly suffer, and that if for three years they neglected music, music must certainly die out – and that seeing nature has taught us that when the old year's grain is finished the new has sprung up for us – seeing also that all the changes[32] in procuring fire by friction have been gone through in the four seasons – surely a twelve-month might suffice.

The Master asked him, "Would it be a satisfaction to you – that returning to better food, that putting on of fine clothes?"

"It would," said he.

"Then if you can be satisfied in so doing, do

---

[32] Different woods were adopted for this purpose at the various seasons.

so. But to a gentleman, who is in mourning for a parent, the choicest food will not be palatable, nor will the listening to music be pleasant, nor will comforts of home make him happy in mind. Hence he does not do as you suggest. But if you are now happy in your mind, then do so."

Tsai Wo went out. And the Master went on to say, "It is want of human feeling in this man. After a child has lived three years it then breaks away from the tender nursing of its parents. And this three years' mourning is the customary mourning prevalent all over the empire. Can this man have enjoyed the three years of loving care from his parents?"

"Ah, it is difficult," said he, "to know what to make of those who are all day long cramming themselves with food and are without anything to apply their minds to! Are there no dice and chess players? Better, perhaps, join in that pursuit than do nothing at all!"

"Does a gentleman," asked Tsz-lu, "make much account of bravery?"

"Righteousness he counts higher," said the Master. "A gentleman who is brave without being just may become turbulent; while a common person who is brave and not just may end in becoming a highwayman."

Tsz-kung asked, "I suppose a gentleman will have his aversions as well as his likings?"

"Yes," replied the Master, "he will dislike those who talk much about other people's ill-deeds. He will dislike those who, when occupying inferior places, utter defamatory words against their superiors. He will dislike those who, though they may be brave, have no regard for propriety. And he will dislike those hastily decisive and venturesome spirits who are nevertheless so hampered by limited intellect."

"And you, too, Tsz-kung," he continued, "have your aversions, have you not?"

"I dislike," said he, "those plagiarists who wish to pass for wise persons. I dislike those people who wish their lack of humility to be taken for bravery. I dislike also those divulgers of secrets who think to be accounted straightforward."

"Of all others," said the Master, "women-servants and men-servants are the most difficult people to have the care of. Approach them in a familiar manner, and they take liberties; keep them at a distance, and they grumble."

Again, "When a man meets with odium at forty, he will do so to the end."

BOOK EIGHTEEN

Good Men in Seclusion – Duke of Chow to His Son

"IN THE REIGN OF THE last king of the Yin dynasty," Confucius I said, "there were three men of philanthropic spirit: – the viscount of Wei, who withdrew from him; the viscount of Ki, who became his bondsman; and Pi-kan, who reproved him and suffered death."

Hwḳi of Liu-hiŠ, who filled the office of

Chief Criminal Judge, was thrice dismissed. A person remarked to him, "Can you not yet bear to withdraw?" He replied, "If I act in a straightforward way in serving men, whither in these days should I go, where I should not be thrice dismissed? Were I to adopt crooked ways in their service, why need I leave the land where my parents dwell?"

Duke King of Ts'i remarked respecting his attitude towards Confucius, "If he is to be treated like the Chief of the Ki family, I cannot do it. I should treat him as somewhere between the Ki and Mang Chiefs. – I am old," he added, "and not competent to avail myself of him."

Confucius, hearing of this, went away.

The Ts'i officials presented to the Court of Lu a number of female musicians. Ki Hwan accepted them, and for three days no Court was held.

Confucius went away.

Tsieh-yu, the madman[33] of Ts'u, was once passing Confucius, singing as he went along. He sang –

"Ha, the phoenix! Ha, the phoenix!
How is Virtue lying prone!
Vain to chide for what is o'er,
Plan to meet what's yet in store.
Let alone! Let alone!
Risky now to serve a throne."

Confucius alighted, wishing to enter into conversation with him; but the man hurried along and left him, and he was therefore unable to get a word with him.

Ch'ang-tsŁ and Kieh-nih[34] were working together on some ploughed land. Confucius was passing by them, and sent Tsz-lu to ask where the ford was.

---

33 He only pretended to be mad, in order to escape being employed in the public service.

34 Two worthies who had abandoned public life, owing to the state of the times.

Ch’ang-tsŁ said, “Who is the person driving the carriage?”

“Confucius,” answered Tsz-lu.

“He of Lu?” he asked.

“The same,” said Tsz-lu.

“He knows then where the ford is,” said he.

Tsz-lu then put his question to Kieh-nih; and the latter asked, “Who are you?”

Tsz-lu gave his name.

“You are a follower of Confucius of Lu, are you not?”

“You are right,” he answered.

“Ah, as these waters rise and overflow their bounds,” said he, “’tis so with all throughout the empire; and who is he that can alter the state of things? And you are a follower of a learned man who withdraws from his chief; had you not better be a follower of such as have forsaken the world?” And he went on with his harrowing, without stopping.

Tsz-lu went and informed his Master of all

this. He was deeply touched, and said, "One cannot herd on equal terms with beasts and birds: if I am not to live among these human folk, then with whom else should I live? Only when the empire is well ordered shall I cease to take part in the work of reformation."

Tsz-lu was following the Master, but had dropped behind on the way, when he encountered an old man with a weed-basket slung on a staff over his shoulder. Tsz-lu inquired of him, "Have you seen my Master, sir?" Said the old man, "Who is your master? – you who never employ your four limbs in laborious work; you who do not know one from another of the five sorts of grain!" And he stuck his staff in the ground, and began his weeding.

Tsz-lu brought his hands together on his breast and stood still.

The old man kept Tsz-lu and lodged him for the night, killed a fowl and prepared some millet, entertained him, and brought his two sons out to see him.

On the morrow Tsz-lu went on his way, and told all this to the Master, who said, "He is a recluse," and sent Tsz-lu back to see him again. But by the time he got there he was gone.

Tsz-lu remarked upon this, "It is not right he should evade official duties. If he cannot allow any neglect of the terms on which elders and juniors should live together, how is it that he neglects to conform to what is proper as between prince and public servant? He wishes for himself personally a pure life, yet creates disorder in that more important relationship. When a gentleman undertakes public work, he will carry out the duties proper to it; and he knows beforehand that right principles may not win their way."

Among those who have retired from public life have been Peh-I and Shuh-Ts'i, Yu-chung, I-yih, Chu-chang, Hwḳi of Liuhia, and ShŠu-lien.

"Of these," said the Master, "Peh-I and

Shuh-Ts'i may be characterized, I should say, as men who never declined from their high resolve nor soiled themselves by aught of disgrace.

"Of Hwḳi of Liu-hiŠ and ShŠu-lien, if one may say that they did decline from high resolve, and that they did bring disgrace upon themselves, yet their words were consonant with established principles, and their action consonant with men's thoughts and wishes; and this is all that may be said of them.

"Of Yu-chung and I-yih, if it be said that when they retired into privacy they let loose their tongues, yet in their aim at personal purity of life they succeeded, and their defection was also successful in its influence.

"My own rule is different from any adopted by these: I will take no liberties, I will have no curtailing of my liberty."

The chief music-master went off to Ts'i. Kan, the conductor of the music at the second repast, went over to Ts'u. LiŠu, conductor at the third repast, went over to Ts'ai. And Kiueh, who conducted at the fourth, went to Ts'in.

Fang-shuh, the drummer, withdrew into the neighborhood of the Ho. Wu the tambourer went to the Han. And Yang the junior music-master, and Siang who played on the musical stone, went to the sea-coast.

Anciently the Duke of Chow, addressing his son the Duke of Lu, said, "A good man in high place is not indifferent about the members of his own family, and does not give occasion to the chief ministers to complain that they are not employed; nor without great cause will he set aside old friendships; nor does he seek for full equipment for every kind of service in any single man."

There were once eight officials during this Chow dynasty, who were four pairs of twins, all brothers – the eldest pair Tab and Kwoh, the next Tub and Hwuh, the third Yt' and HiŠ, the youngest Sui and Kwa.

BOOK NINETEEN

Teachings of Various Chief Disciples

"THE LEARNED OFFICIAL," said Tsz-chang, "who when he sees danger ahead will risk his very life, who when he sees a chance of success is mindful of what is just and proper, who in his religious acts is mindful of the duty of reverence, and when in mourning thinks of his loss, is indeed a fit and proper person for his place."

Again he said, "If a person hold to virtue but never advance in it, and if he have faith in right principles and do not build himself up in them, how can he be regarded either as having such, or as being without them?"

Tsz-hiŠ's disciples asked Tsz-chang his views about intercourse with others. "What says your Master?" he rejoined. "He says," they replied, "'Associate with those who are qualified, and repel from you such as are not.'" Tsz-chang then said, "That is different from what I have learnt. A superior man esteems the worthy and wise, and bears with all. He makes much of the good and capable, and pities the incapable. Am I eminently worthy and wise? – who is there then among men whom I will not bear with? Am I not worthy and wise? – others will be minded to repel me: I have nothing to do with repelling them."

Sayings of Tsz-hiŠ: –

"Even in inferior pursuits there must be something worthy of contemplation, but if carried to an extreme there is danger of fanaticism; hence the superior man does not engage in them.

"The student who daily recognizes how much he yet lacks, and as the months pass forgets not what he has succeeded in learning, may undoubtedly be called a lover of learning.

"Wide research and steadfast purpose, eager questioning and close reflection – all this tends to humanize a man.

"As workmen spend their time in their workshops for the perfecting of their work, so superior men apply their minds to study in order to make themselves thoroughly conversant with their subjects.

"When an inferior man does a wrong thing, he is sure to gloss it over.

"The superior man is seen in three different aspects: – look at him from a distance, he is imposing in appearance; approach him, he is gentle and warm-hearted; hear him speak, he is acute and strict.

"Let such a man have the people's confidence, and he will get much work out of them; so long, however, as he does not possess their confidence they will regard him as grinding them down.

"When confidence is reposed in him, he may then with impunity administer reproof; so long as it is not, he will be regarded as a detractor.

"Where there is no over-stepping of barriers in the practice of the higher virtues, there may be freedom to pass in and out in the practice of the lower ones."

Tsz-yu had said, "The pupils in the school of Tsz-hiŠ are good enough at such things as sprinkling and scrubbing floors, answering calls and replying to questions from superiors, and advancing and retiring to and from such; but these things are only offshoots – as to the root of things they are nowhere. What is the use of all that?"

When this came to the ears of Tsz-hiŠ, he said, "Ah! there he is mistaken. What does a master, in his methods of teaching, consider first in his precepts? And what does he account next, as that about which he may be indifferent? It is like as in the study of plants – classification by **differentiae**. How may a master play fast and loose in his methods of instruction? Would they not indeed be sages, who could take in at once the first principles and the final developments of things?"

Further observations of Tsz-hiŠ: –

"In the public service devote what energy and time remain to study. After study devote what energy and time remain to the public service.

"As to the duties of mourning, let them cease when the grief is past.

"My friend Tsz-chang, although he has the ability to tackle hard things, has not yet the virtue of philanthropy."

The learned Tsang observed, "How loftily Tsz-chang bears himself! Difficult indeed along with him to practise philanthropy!"

Again he said, "I have heard this said by

the Master, that 'though men may not exert themselves to the utmost in other duties, yet surely in the duty of mourning for their parents they will do so!'"

Again, "This also I have heard said by the Master: 'The filial piety of Mang Chwang in other respects might be equalled, but as manifested in his making no changes among his father's ministers, nor in his father's mode of government – that aspect of it could not easily be equalled.'"

Yang Fu, having been made senior Criminal Judge by the Chief of the Mang clan, consulted with the learned Tsang. The latter advised him as follows: "For a long time the Chiefs have failed in their government, and the people have become unsettled. When you arrive at the facts of their cases, do not rejoice at your success in that, but rather be sorry for them, and have pity upon them."

Tsz-kung once observed, "We speak of 'the iniquity of ChŠu' – but 'twas not so great as this. And so it is that the superior man is averse from settling in this sink, into which everything runs that is foul in the empire."

Again he said, "Faults in a superior man are like eclipses of the sun or moon: when he is guilty of a trespass men all see it; and when he is himself again, all look up to him."

Kung-sun Ch'an of Wei inquired of Tsz-kung how Confucius acquired his learning.

Tsz-kung replied, "The teachings of Wan and Wu have not yet fallen to the ground. They exist in men. Worthy and wise men have the more important of these stored up in their minds; and others, who are not such, store up the less important of them; and as no one is thus without the teachings of Wan and Wu, how should our Master not have learned? And moreover what permanent preceptor could he have?"

Shuh-sun Wu-shuh, addressing the high officials at the Court, remarked that Tsz-kung was a greater worthy than Confucius.

Tsz-fuh King-pih went and informed Tsz-kung of this remark.

Tsz-kung said, "Take by way of comparison the walls outside our houses. My wall is shoulder-high, and you may look over it and see what the house and its contents are worth. My Master's wall is tens of feet high, and unless you should effect an entrance by the door, you would fail to behold the beauty of the ancestral hall and the rich array of all its officers. And they who effect an entrance by the door, methinks, are few! Was it not, however, just like him – that remark of the Chief?"

Shuh-sun Wu-shuh had been casting a slur on the character of Confucius.

"No use doing that," said Tsz-kung; "he is irreproachable. The wisdom and worth of other men are little hills and mounds of earth: traversible. He is the sun, or the moon, impossible to reach and pass. And what harm, I ask, can a man do to the sun or the moon, by wishing to intercept himself from either? It all shows that he knows not how to gauge capacity."

Tsz-k'in, addressing Tsz-kung, said, "You depreciate yourself. Confucius is surely not a greater worthy than yourself."

Tsz-kung replied, "In the use of words one ought never to be incautious; because a gentleman for one single utterance of his is apt to be considered a wise man, and for a single utterance may be accounted unwise. No more might one think of attaining to the Master's perfections than think of going upstairs to Heaven! Were it ever his fortune to be at the head of the government of a country, then that which is spoken of as 'establishing the country' would be establishment indeed; he would be its guide and it would follow him, he would tranquillize it and it would render its willing homage: he would give forward impulses to it to which it would harmoniously respond. In his life he would be its glory, at his death there would be great lamentation. How indeed could such as he be equalled?"

BOOK TWENTY

Extracts from the Book of History

THE EMPEROR YAU SAID to Shun, "Ah, upon you, upon your person, lies the Heaven-appointed order of succession! Faithfully hold to it, without any deflection; for if within the four seas necessity and want befall the people, your own revenue will forever come to an end."

Shun also used the same language in handing down the appointment to Yu.

The Emperor T'ang in his prayer, said, "I, the child Li, presume to avail me of an ox of dusky hue, and presume to manifestly announce to Thee, O God, the most high and Sovereign Potentate, that to the transgressor I dare not grant forgiveness, nor yet keep in abeyance Thy ministers. Judgment rests in Thine heart, O God. Should we ourself transgress, may the guilt not be visited everywhere upon all. Should the people all transgress, be the guilt upon ourself!"

Chow possessed great gifts, by which the able and good were richly endowed.

"Although," said King Wu, "he is surrounded by his near relatives, they are not to be compared with men of humane spirit. The people are suffering wrongs, and the remedy rests with me – the one man."

After Wu had given diligent attention to the

various weights and measures, examined the laws and regulations, and restored the degraded officials, good government everywhere ensued.

He caused ruined States to flourish again, reinstated intercepted heirs, and promoted to office men who had gone into retirement; and the hearts of the people throughout the empire drew towards him.

Among matters of prime consideration with him were these – food for the people, the duty of mourning, and sacrificial offerings to the departed.

He was liberal and large-hearted, and so won all hearts; true, and so was trusted by the people; energetic, and thus became a man of great achievements; just in his rule, and all were well content.

Tsz-chang in a conversation with Confucius asked, "What say you is essential for the proper conduct of government?"

The Master replied, "Let the ruler hold in high estimation the five excellences, and eschew the four evils; then may he conduct his government properly."

"And what call you the five excellences?" he was asked.

"They are," he said, "Bounty without extravagance; burdening without exciting discontent; desire without covetousness; dignity without haughtiness; show of majesty without fierceness."

"What mean you," asked Tsz-chang, "by bounty without extravagance?"

"Is it not this," he replied – "to make that which is of benefit to the people still more beneficial? When he selects for them such labors as it is possible for them to do, and exacts them, who will then complain? So when his desire is the virtue of humaneness, and he attains it, how shall he then be covetous? And if – whether he have to do with few or with many, with small or with great – he do not venture ever to be careless, is not this also to have dignity without haughtiness? And if – when properly vested in robe and cap, and showing dignity in his every look – his appearance be so imposing that the people look up to and stand in awe of him, is not this moreover to show majesty without fierceness?"

"What, then, do you call the four evils?" said Tsz-chang.

The answer here was, "Omitting to instruct the people and then inflicting capital punishment on them – which means cruel tyranny. Omitting to give them warning and yet looking for perfection in them – which means oppression. Being slow and late in issuing requisitions, and exacting strict punctuality in the returns – which means robbery. And likewise, in intercourse with men, to expend and to receive in a stingy manner – which is to act the part of a mere commissioner."

"None can be a superior man," said the Master, "who does not recognize the decrees of Heaven.

"None can have stability in him without a knowledge of the proprieties.

"None can know a man without knowing his utterances."

www.ingramcontent.com/pod-product-compliance
Lightning Source LLC
Chambersburg PA
CBHW020913310726
48980CB00011B/864/J

* 9 7 8 1 8 3 4 1 2 2 8 2 3 *